SLOB PROOF!

Real-Life **Design Solutions**

SLOB PROOF!

Real-Life Design Solutions

Debbie Wiener

A

ALPHA

A member of Penguin Group (USA)

ALPHA BOOKS

Published by the Penguin Group

Penguin Group (USA) Inc., 375 Hudson Street, New York, New York 10014, USA

Penguin Group (Canada), 90 Eglinton Avenue East, Suite 700, Toronto, Ontario M4P 2Y3, Canada (a division of Pearson Penguin Canada Inc.)

Penguin Books Ltd., 80 Strand, London WC2R 0RL, England

Penguin Ireland, 25 St. Stephen's Green, Dublin 2, Ireland (a division of Penguin Books Ltd.)

Penguin Group (Australia), 250 Camberwell Road, Camberwell, Victoria 3124, Australia (a division of Pearson Australia Group Pty. Ltd.)

Penguin Books India Pvt. Ltd., 11 Community Centre, Panchsheel Park, New Delhi—110 017, India

Penguin Group (NZ), 67 Apollo Drive, Rosedale, North Shore, Auckland 1311, New Zealand (a division of Pearson New Zealand Ltd.)

Penguin Books (South Africa) (Pty.) Ltd., 24 Sturdee Avenue, Rosebank, Johannesburg 2196, South Africa

Penguin Books Ltd., Registered Offices: 80 Strand, London WC2R 0RL, England

International Standard Book Number: 978-1-59257-769-9
Library of Congress Catalog Card Number: 2008924714

10   09   08   8   7   6   5   4   3   2   1

Interpretation of the printing code: The rightmost number of the first series of numbers is the year of the book's printing; the rightmost number of the second series of numbers is the number of the book's printing. For example, a printing code of 08-1 shows that the first printing occurred in 2008.

Printed in the United States of America

Most Alpha books are available at special quantity discounts for bulk purchases for sales promotions, premiums, fund-raising, or educational use. Special books, or book excerpts, can also be created to fit specific needs.

For details, write: Special Markets, Alpha Books, 375 Hudson Street, New York, NY 10014.

This book is dedicated to my own slobs, Jim, Sam, and Jacob.
I love you—now wipe your feet!
And to my dad, who taught me to always look under the covers.
I miss you.

Contents

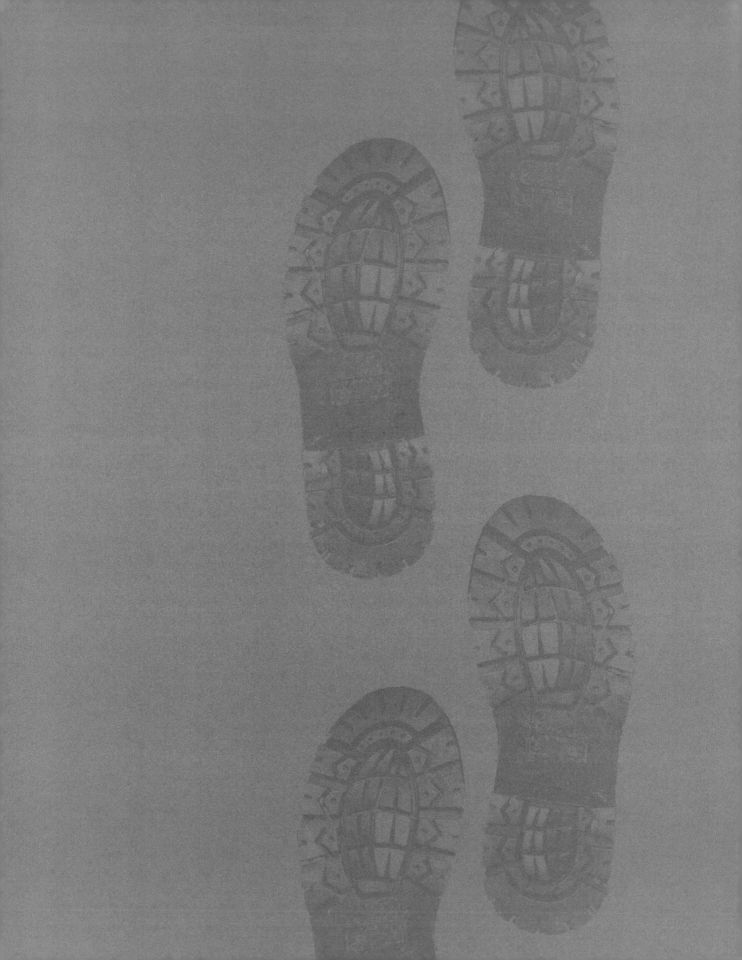

Introduction

All you Homer and Marge Simpsons out there, listen up! I wrote this book for you. It's not that I'm such a big *Simpsons* fan (although I do love the show), but I live with my own Homer. His name is Jim and he's a slob.

I'm an interior designer—I've been doing it for almost 15 years. Furniture is in my blood. My dad ran a mattress factory that also made custom upholstery for area furniture stores and designers. I spent part of every weekend of my childhood accompanying my dad to furniture stores and learning how furniture is styled and made.

I didn't write a book about pretty rooms; I wrote about comfortable, durable rooms that can hold up to the way many people really live. My design tips are for the cleaning-impaired, the decorating-challenged, and those of us who'd rather sit on the furniture than protect it from being sat on.

I have no gimmicks. I'm not an actress. I've certainly never been a model. I'm not famous, I have no furniture line, and I don't lead a glamorous or sexy life. There's nothing hip or chic about me. I just tell it the way it really is.

It's all about time. We don't have enough of it. Between work, school, and family—not to mention laundry and an occasional home-cooked meal—I lost the time it takes to dress and style my home. I don't have time to even care. Most of us run out of the house with dirty dishes in the sink, laundry piled up in the hall, and beds unmade. Most of us aren't around to check if shoes are off the furniture or coasters are placed under drinks.

If you're most of us, this is your book!

I love to look through home design magazines. Who doesn't love that perfectly cream-colored room with flowing curtains, straight chairs, and coffee tables laden with coffee-table books? It's art—but it's not real life. Great to look at but not to live in. It's like falling in love with the wrong man—he looks so good; you love him, you want him, but you know deep down inside … you can't *live* with him!

Real-life design isn't art—it's smart!

Why am I doing this? I didn't start off as a designer obsessed with slob-proofing my home. I married into this. I started out in life like many of my generation, with a mom who was concerned only with how things looked—how she looked, how we looked, and how our family home looked. There was no concern for how we felt. Our home was intended for the outside world. It was pristine, decorated in the 1970s by the top designer in Boston and highly styled, all at the cost of our comfort and peace of mind. Our home was always ready for that make-believe magazine editor who might show up at any time and shoot our home. I was destined to repeat the pattern of keeping up appearances, and when I decorated my marital home, it was all about how things looked. Early in my marriage, I set down the law when it came to eating out of the kitchen, wiping your feet at the door, and using coasters under drinks. Before anyone came to dinner, I revacuumed, refluffed, and reprimped so that rooms looked like pages from magazines that no one had ever set foot in.

In so many ways, my husband did me a big favor. He released my inner slob, who was just dying to put her shoes on the ottoman or cut an apple directly on the countertop. We still have company for dinner several times a month. But now, to get ready, I merely flush the toilets before guests arrive and put out clean hand towels. My home looks good enough. Best of all, my friends and my kids' friends are at ease in my house and, most important, so is my family. Now, isn't that the whole point of having and furnishing a home in the first place? We so infrequently get to sit together, eat together, or relax together, it's no longer important that the room look perfect. It matters only that we're all together. Create comfortable spaces for you, your family, and your friends, and they will come. How do you get rid of them after a few days? We'll cover that in my next book.

What follows are my tried-and-true recommendations for decorating your home with furnishings that will look good longer and stay comfortable no matter who lives in it. I focus on the essential stuff that takes the greatest abuse—flooring, seating, windows, and walls, with advice on how to add color and lighting to all of it. I'm not an advocate for buying cheap stuff and replacing it every couple of years—I'm all for buying something once and knowing that it will hold up to the way you really live. So at the end of each chapter, I've added my favorite lines— from manufacturers I have used and can vouch for. Since many of these aren't available directly to consumers, you may have to ask your local retailer if they carry my recommendations.

At the end of a long and busy day, who cares if your kids forget to wipe their shoes, or if your husband spills something on the family room sofa, or if your dog has an accident? Make your home work for you instead of you working for your home. Be prepared for whatever your family throws at or on your home furnishings. Make it slob proof!

Acknowledgments

Thank you to those who have helped me over the years:

A special thanks to my friends at the Washington Design Center—Jason Pail, Wayne Breeden, Christopher Greer, Deborah Hassan, Doug Hartsell, and Julia Chappell—for the support you've shown me over the years and the many opportunities you've shared with me.

To Mel Lowe and Linda Gombos, my longtime lighting team, for the hard work, dedication, and your help with hundreds of projects we've lit up over the years. You light up my life!

To Ellen Jacobson, my color expert, decorative painter, artist, and friend. Thanks for always being there to roll up your sleeves and help.

To Barbara Sweeney and Anne Gummerson for their great photography and support. To Mark Finkenstaedt, my extraordinary photographer. Thank you, Mark, for sharing your intuitive sense of lighting and color, and bringing all this design work to life. I couldn't look this good without your dedication, vision, and artistry.

A special thanks to my friend and magazine editor, Sherry Moeller, for your great advice and your support, as always. And to Annie Groer, Trish Donnally, Jennifer Sergent, Dennis Hockman, and Sharon Dan, for the positive feedback you've given me time and again.

To my friends and colleagues at Penguin—Randy Ladenheim-Gil, Executive Editor, and Becky Harmon, Designer—thanks so much for the professionalism, dedication, creative insight, and publishing expertise that made this book happen.

Most of all, thank you, Kim Prati, the best graphic designer I know. No one can do the visuals like you, Kim! I can't thank you enough for the countless hours, the late nights, and all the weekends you spent sorting through photos and laying out the text—I couldn't have done this book without you, Kim!

Chapter 1

GET FLOORED

It all started on the floor. I remember vividly the day my husband spilled an entire cup of coffee, with half and half in it, on my beautiful, beige carpeted stairs. It was the day before Thanksgiving, and company was coming in about 12 hours. I had a conniption looking at that big spot of hot coffee, simultaneously screaming at my husband and doing everything I knew to mop up the growing stain. I almost called a divorce attorney—I couldn't have been more upset than if my husband had just confessed that he'd been leading a double life, with another wife and children in a nearby town. To a serious design aficionado like myself, the coffee spill was worse.

Fifteen years later, we're still married—happily, I might add. The coffee stain, which never came out, is long gone. In fact, there isn't a speck of beige carpet to be found in my home. All is well now because I learned that even the best-laid foundation is subject to change, especially when you live with a slob.

Laying the Groundwork

My husband grew up in Manhattan in a big building right on Park Avenue. Looking at him now with his shirttail hanging out, his shoes untied, the day's lunch staining the front of his shirt, his fly barely zipped, and a baseball cap on his head, it's hard to believe. When he came home from school, he walked through a carpeted lobby easily 300 feet in length before he even reached the carpeted elevator up to his family's seventh-floor apartment. Whatever came into the building on the soles of his shoes was gone by the time he reached the apartment door—without any effort. So my husband never learned to wipe his feet! No one ever told him to do it.

stair runner

colorful foyer rug

A foyer rug and stair runner dark enough to camouflage daily dirt will go a long way toward preserving your sanity.

Photo by Anne Gummerson

FLOORS

natural
slate
tile

colorful
patterned
rug

Natural slate tile with colorful, patterned wool area rugs on top combine to make durable, cleanable slob-proof flooring.

Photo by Mark Finkenstaedt

FLOORS

Dirt Detectors

The walk from the driveway to our door is much shorter than the one my husband was used to as a child, and there's no carpet, just flagstone. So everything on my husband's shoes is still on them when he enters the house. It has been my dream since the day we moved in to install flashing neon signs on motion detectors that turn on and glare like stadium lighting, instructing him to wipe his feet on the front door mat. Okay, so I haven't done it yet, but my ears have been trained over time to recognize the sound of his car pulling up the driveway so that I can meet him at the door and yell, "Wipe your feet!"

Just wiping your feet at the door will keep your floors cleaner and looking good longer. But don't assume that everyone visiting or living in your home with dirty shoes will think to do this—so put a thick, oversized mat at each door. People will be forced to walk on it and wipe up without giving it a thought. And if your kids come in and take off their shoes, their friends will follow suit.

It doesn't always work. I'm not always there in time. During the fall, when leaves cover the ground, the mess in the foyer is unbelievable and it gets tracked everywhere—upstairs, downstairs, even into the bathroom. Even though I have grown accustomed to the sound of crunching leaves whenever and wherever we walk in the house, this is where a "take-your-shoes-off-at-the-door" policy could really make a difference.

To begin the slob-proofing process, start where all great civilizations have in the past—from the ground up.

The Power of Patterns

Since constant nagging to "Wipe your feet!" is tiring for me as well as my husband, I've learned to outsmart him—in many ways, which, being a woman, ain't so hard to do. First, I added a large 3'×5' polypropylene indoor/outdoor rug on the front porch. It looks good, and he can't help but walk on it as he approaches the door. It's just plush enough to remove a lot of dirt from the soles of his shoes. This rug is my first line of defense.

Next, I got rid of the beautiful but neutral-colored runner that once looked so good—for exactly 24 hours, I mean—on our foyer and hall floor. I replaced it with two smaller matching rugs in chocolate brown with bursts of green, orange, and turquoise in a highly patterned design.

These rugs camouflage everything coming into the house, and permanent stains blend in so well that only I know they're there. Matching the foyer's area rugs to the color of dirt was a sanity-saving move for me. They keep my entryway looking good, and they're small enough to be removed every now and then for professional cleaning. I should add here that my husband never even noticed when I made the rug switch—he only noticed that I stopped nagging him to wipe his feet. That was good enough for him. (There's more on area rugs for the rest of the home later in the chapter.)

Color is a young girl's best friend—on the chair fabric, on the curtains, and especially on the floor.
Photo by Mark Finkenstaedt

colorful
curtains

colorful
fabric on
chair

colorful
patterned
rug

Color and pattern are your best weapons in the daily war against your slobs. In wool rugs, color and pattern provide unbeatable durability, softness, and style.
Photos by Mark Finkenstaedt

We took the pattern out of the rug and created a matching backsplash– what's good for the floor is good for the wall!

Photo by Randy Sager

pattern from backsplash

pattern from rug

FLOORS

Just Say No

Since every spill, every spot, and everything on your shoes stays on the floor until it's cleaned, it's important to make flooring decisions based on both the ability to camouflage dirt and durability. Choosing carefully is not just good design sense; it's a major budgetary decision as well.

My number one rule about all flooring is "No neutrals!" No beige, cream, light taupe or butter yellow, off-white, pale silver, white wash or antique cream, or buttermilk. As you'll see in the photos throughout this book, not every client listens. One day in the not-too-distant future, design anthropologists will look back at our homes and laugh at how many of us, myself included, were stupid enough to choose beige carpet, bisque tile, and light wood floors. Why? These neutrals are dying breeds because they cannot withstand heavy use, dirty shoes, and the daily dust that fills an average home. Neutrals require care and vigilance to stay clean and look good. When you have beige carpet, it's like having another child in the house!

Photo by Anne Gummerson

Photo by Mark Finkenstaedt

Even if you prefer geometrics over abstract patterns, you can still choose vibrant colors and just say no to neutrals!

Long Live Wood

Which floor should you start with underneath the area rug? Wood is my favorite choice, and in my house, there's hardwood throughout the bedrooms and living spaces. Where hardwood didn't exist, I added it, then protected it by placing soft, colorful area rugs on top.

Why wood? Hardwood never goes out of style and is still the most popular choice for flooring in new and old homes. Hardwood adds value and luxury to every room because it's a natural material, not as hard underfoot as stone or tile, richer than synthetic man-made materials, and more versatile than even the best-quality wall-to-wall broadloom carpet.

Given how long it lasts and its ability to be refinished, hardwood is a good value when you consider its cost over the life of your home. Hardwood comes in every price range and style—it's amazing how the choices have expanded so that it's more affordable and accessible than ever.

Price Points Versus Types

Are you thinking of putting hardwood in your home? At the lowest price range, there's oak—readily available in every plank size and stain finish. On the higher end, there are exotic, even sustainable choices, such as Brazilian Cherry, Jahoba, Wenge, and Zebra woods, many of which are actually harder than traditional oak floors. The harder the wood, the more resistant it is to signs of scratching and wear and tear. But even a lower-priced oak floor is more than durable enough for a typical family.

A wood with good *graining* shows less dirt than one like maple, which has a smooth, consistent finish. Dings and scratches from toys, sport cleats, and pets are much less likely to stand out on a distressed wood floor— an unevenness that gives an older look to a new floor — which works in both traditional and contemporary homes. If dents and scratches are your problem, a distressed wood like hickory is a perfect choice.

Graining: The distinctive appearance and pattern inherent in most types of wood.

If the price of exotic hardwoods is out of reach, look at bamboo, which is available in dozens of different colors with unique graining at relatively inexpensive prices (around $6 to $8 per square foot—about the same as good wall-to-wall carpet). It comes ready to sand and stain in any color you would use on other unfinished

natural
oak flooring

Natural oak flooring is inherently slob proof. It's easy to clean, easy
to touch up, and, just like your face, will age with character!
Photo by Mark Finkenstaedt

Hardness Rating

Type	Rating	$$$
American Black Cherry	950	moderate
Brazilian Cherry	2820	high

wood floors or with a hard-wearing, scratch-resistant factory finish. Best of all, it's a sustainable, green design choice because it regrows rapidly. You see, it's not wood—it's grass! Very, very hard grass. I love the graining in bamboo—the striped effect that's common in bamboo flooring provides great camouflage for pet hair, dirt, and dust. And if you can't see it, who cares if it's there?

Prefinished or Finished in Place

If you don't have wood floors now, getting hardwood into your home can be messy and inconvenient, not to mention costly. Traditionally, hardwood is installed unfinished and then the planks are sanded and stained on-site. The sanding leaves a thin residue of dust everywhere—and you must stay off the floor during installation, staining, and finishing, which can take several days. But laying hardwood this way gives you the most long-term options for changing the color of your floor and repairing it after your kids grow up and leave home. Even a kitchen floor battered by scrubbing, scratching, and heavy use can look new overnight with sanding and refinishing. Plus, because the floors were all done at one time, the look will be seamless and smooth, with a continuous finish that ties the whole floor together. It reduces the transitions—places where you see a strip of wood or metal—from room to room.

Prefinished hardwoods and engineered hardwoods are a faster, cleaner way to add hardwood to your home. My one complaint about them is those darn beveled edges (these are the little recessed gaps between each plank), which are a necessary evil—they allow the easy installation that makes prefinished flooring a popular option, but they also trap dirt that's hard to get out.

Photo by Barbara Sweeney

Shine or No Shine

The finish you choose for your hardwood is as important as the paint you use on your walls. Who would choose wall paint in a home with slobs that isn't scrubbable and long wearing? Well, it's the same for hardwood flooring. Some finishes are better choices than others. A high-gloss ebony stain, which I admit is absolutely gorgeous to look at, shows more dust and scratches than a lighter brown stain or a natural, satin-finish wood floor with no stain.

FLOORS

Glossy finishes show imperfections, and the shiny, reflective surface in polyurethane showcases every speck of dust. A matte or satin surface isn't reflective and conceals imperfections and dirt better.

What do you see now on your floor? Consider the color of the hair, spots, and stains you're living with now, and factor that into any future flooring decisions.

Take Care

Wood is a natural product, like the skin on your face. Both need protection from the sun and abuse. No matter how much care you take, both will show signs of aging over time—it's inevitable. Lines and wrinkles add character and distinction to a person's face; family life will also add character to your wood floor! Dirt, grit, and moisture are your hardwood floor's worst enemies, and they'll age your flooring investment quickly without the necessary protection. Natural wood with no stain or wood with a medium-toned stain holds up best over time. Why? Abrasion, scrubbing, and daily wear break down a floor's surface, and the first thing to wear off is the stain. The more closely the surface matches the wood underneath, the longer this aging process takes. Area rugs at doors and around the kitchen floor are essential. Consider a large, textured grass mat or indoor/outdoor rug to ensure that even the most thoughtless person wipes their feet before entering your home.

Pets can also age a floor quickly. Cat and dog nails can scratch and gouge your hardwood. Some manufacturers recommend that you put booties on your pets, or at least cut their nails. The question is, who do you love more—your dog, your cat, or your floor? I think most true pet lovers learn to live with their dinged and dented wood floors. Again, it's all "character"!

Check your kitchen table and chairs periodically for scratching and wear on the kitchen floor. In my house, this is where the most damage is caused, with chairs pulled out and pushed in several times a day. Keep plenty of sticky felt pads on hand to protect your floor in high-use areas.

Natural wood with no stain or wood with a medium-toned stain holds up best over time. Why? Abrasion, scrubbing, and daily wear break down a floor's surface, and the first thing to wear off is the stain. The more closely the surface matches the wood underneath, the longer this aging process will take.

Since pooling water also damages hardwood floors, wipe up spills quickly. Again, a thick rug in front of kitchen and powder room sinks and in front of wet areas will go a long way toward protecting your wood floor.

Resilient Flooring

Not too long ago, I wouldn't even consider *resilient flooring* for anyone's home, unless it was for the basement storage area or a laundry room. It was just too cheap and artificial looking. Sure, every home had vinyl flooring, but we designers turned up our noses at Mannington no-wax floors and wouldn't have anything to do with them.

Old resilient flooring had tile seams that darkened with age, looking dated, dirty, and worn.
Photo by Designing Solutions

Resilient Flooring: Vinyl, linoleum, and cork flooring with give and bounce

dark aged tile

BEFORE

The latest technology offers new textures, colors, and finishes that more closely resemble wood and stone than before. Some of them can really fool you. Consumers and designers alike perceive resilient flooring materials, including the big names like Pergo and Congoleum, as a low-end flooring choice. Like I said, I'm guilty of this prejudice myself: I always prefer the real thing in a home to a synthetic imitation.

But resilient flooring adds convenience, and therein lies its value and popularity. It remains a pet-, slob-, and kid-friendly choice that's easy to install, requires no care or maintenance, and costs less than the real thing. As a general rule, the more you spend on it, the more realistic it looks and the longer the warranty, so go with the top of the line. Resilient flooring is made to withstand abuse and bounce back without any damage. The stuff has merit—it's a real workhorse.

If resilient flooring is the right choice for you, take a look at Marmoleum. I love this product because it doesn't pretend to be stone or wood. It's a natural linoleum floor that's made with 100 percent natural ingredients: linseed oil, cork, limestone, tree resin, and natural minerals. Because it's natural, it looks totally different from other resilient floor choices yet shares the same hard-wearing properties. The colors, large-size sheets, and ease of cutting the material allow you to create more unusual shapes and patterns. It's not as inexpensive as other resilient floor choices, but it's not synthetic, so it's a green choice that adds a more natural look to your flooring.

FLOORS

no ugly dark seams

AFTER

The redesigned kitchen still has resilient flooring, but new technology makes the tile seams virtually invisible. The darker accent tiles are placed randomly for a more natural look.
Photo by Anne Gummerson

DuraCeramic tile makes slob-proof flooring soft, quiet, and less slippery than ordinary ceramic tile. It's virtually indestructible, too.
Photos by Congoleum, www.congoleum.com

Pergo, Fausfloor, and other synthetic wood floors are a great choice for basements and play rooms, where value, resilience, low maintenance, and durability are the overriding factors. It's perfect for basements and lower levels because moisture doesn't affect this flooring. DuraCeramic from Congoleum and Fausfloor flooring make a great alternative to more expensive ceramic and stone tile. They're offered in varied sizes, and you can install them with or without grout. If you stick to the simple finishes that don't try to look like marble, the floor will look more authentic.

Marmoleum makes slob-proofing "green" with colorful floor tiles made from natural ingredients.

Photos by Forbo, www.themarmoleumstore.com

FLOORS

Porcelain and Ceramic Tiles

Tile flooring is growing in popularity and in size. Where 10"×10" tiles were once the norm, 18"×36" rectangles fit newer, larger kitchens and master bathrooms better. Rectangular tiles are best laid in offset patterns, resembling bricks. It's more dramatic, giving smaller rooms a feeling of greater space. I always find that the less a floor pattern repeats, the larger the floor looks. And there's a great advantage to using these larger tiles—less grout to clean.

Photo by Designing Solutions

BEFORE

Photo by Mark Finkenstaedt

AFTER

puppy-friendly tile

Tile is a dog's—and a dog lover's—best friend.

When it comes to tile, porcelain is as close to indestructible as you can get. Fired at very high temperatures, porcelain tiles are impervious to water and are the most durable and easiest to clean because of their unique hardness. Ceramic tiles are fired at a lower temperature and have a glaze on the surface, making them a bit softer and less durable than porcelain, but easier to cut and install. Some ceramics can't be used in outdoor locations (like an unheated sunroom or porch) and some shouldn't be used in bathrooms because of their water absorption rates. If you go with ceramic, make sure you choose tiles that are suited to the room.

Both porcelain and ceramic can mimic natural stone and, because of their glazing and high-temperature firing, don't need sealing, like the real stuff … stone.

Stone Tiles

There we were, on our family's first trip to the Holy Land—Israel. Our bus full of tourists stopped at one of a dozen archaeological sites. But this one was different for me. I walked through this tourist site and stopped dead in my tracks. The place was full of mosaic tile … itsy bitsy tiles depicting colorful scenes from literally thousands of years ago. The colors were vibrant, the tiles intact. I couldn't get past the fact that these stones had survived over the centuries. A miracle, perhaps? Yes! Do you know how hard it is to find a good tile installer?

When I chose tile to remodel my bath—and my bath is truly like the public restroom in a bus depot—I used slate. Heck, if stone can survive over the millennia with no door mats, periodic sealing, or flashing signs telling the ancient Israelites to wipe their feet, it should make it through the next 20 years in my bathroom.

Despite what contractors will tell you, natural stone flooring will hold up. Unlike glazed ceramic tiles or porcelain, stone tiles don't have a protective glazed coating on top, and the color goes all the way through the tile. Stone is porous, and it needs to be sealed before installation with a silicone product that actually penetrates the tile. After installation, it should be cleaned using a pH-balanced cleaner

Photo by Mark Finkenstaedt

stone tiles

FLOORS

stone
tiles

If stone tile can make it through millennia, it can survive in your bathroom, too.
Photo by Anne Gummerson

When I suggest a marble, travertine, limestone, or other stone floor to clients, they think it will be too delicate and too absorbent, and require too much care. So I ask them where they work. Many name an office building that's 40 years old, and if they do, I ask if they noticed the marble floor in the lobby. Stone is in more commercial lobbies than any other material. In fact, stone is used to build the building! If it can last in hotels and office buildings, I can't imagine why it won't work in your home. Even if you forget to get it periodically sealed, how bad can it look?

designed specifically for stone floors; a layer of sealant also should be applied annually, whether the floor looks like it needs it or not. If your stone floor becomes dull, scratched, or discolored, call a pro who knows how to restore it for you. You can find a stone flooring specialist in the Yellow Pages by looking under "marble and terrazzo cleaning and service."

FLOORS

marble floor

thick rug

coordinating stair runner

The white marble that came with this house is tough to preserve in the foyer, but it can be protected with a thick wool rug and coordinating runner.
Photo by Anne Gummerson

The five most common stone flooring tiles are these:

Marble: It has been around for centuries, and since no two pieces are exactly alike, you get a finished, distinctive floor that looks natural and elegant. Many colors are routinely stocked in home stores, so marble tile can be a great bargain and a quick way to add elegance in a foyer or bathroom. The most common colors are white, gray, brown-pink, and green-black, generally with a light color background and a darker veining pattern in white and gold. Marble tile usually comes polished, but because it can be slippery when wet, honed marble is a better choice in bathrooms.

Granite: Granite is one of the hardest and most durable of all stones used in flooring. You even see it in city streets—used for curbs. The speckled colorations, all containing some degree of gray, create a subtle pattern of color. Like marble, no two pieces are alike. It's not as formal as marble, and, to be honest, I don't like it on floors—it looks too much like a kitchen countertop!

Slate: This is the most rustic, organic-looking floor tile, made of fine-grained rock with traces of metal. Color variations are inherent in slate and range from lighter taupes and terra cottas to dark charcoal gray and blue. Its earthy look, nonslip surface, and affordable pricing (often starting at $2 per square foot) make it appealing in every room of the house and in every style of home. Use it in a large area, like a foyer, hall, or kitchen. You can mix it up and get a great-looking floor that's also great at masking spots and dirt. (Remember that multicolored carpet is best at masking wear, and the same is true of multicolored slate floor tiles.)

Travertine: With varying degrees of color, ranging from soft white to deep mahogany, travertine is pitted with holes and sometimes veins, giving it an ancient, worn look. You can purchase travertine tile with this old, distressed look or filled, with a smooth, polished surface. I like it old and distressed—it makes me look younger!

Limestone: This is along the same line as travertine—but without the fissures and pock marks. Limestone is very warm-looking and typically pale in color—off-white to cream to golden beige and brown or pink. It comes mottled (with a swirl of lighter color mixed in) or solid in appearance, with a honed or matte finish. Like marble, it can be slippery when wet.

Whichever you choose, porcelain, ceramic, or stone tile, all have one thing in common—they need to be grouted. Grout is simply a mixture of sand, cement, and water that fills the lines and cavities between tiles and creates a water-resistant barrier when dry and hard. It comes in about 40 different colors and can be chosen to blend in or stand out against the tile. Grout is the worst thing about adding floor tile in your home! It discolors, gets mildewy, and makes the expensive tile on your floor look awful. It requires regular cleaning, scrubbing, and sealant, and frankly, I hate the stuff. Your slob will ruin your grout.

I insist on epoxy grout for all tiled surfaces. It's made of resin and hardeners, with no water. I don't actually know what this means, but I do know that epoxy grout gives you outstanding stain resistance, hardness, and durability, so it's the best choice for kitchen counters, floors, and other heavy-traffic areas. You'll never have to scrub it; it won't show mildew and staining, and will keep your tile floor looking good longer. Epoxy grout is expensive—as much as $8 per pound, compared with $1 to $2 for cement-based grout. But because it's impervious to most chemicals and stains, it's well worth the extra cost. You should insist on it, too. If your installer doesn't work with it, find another one who does.

If you're adding tile to a bathroom floor and there are any men or boys—or men who behave like boys—living in your home, or if you're hoping that in the future there may be a man living in your home, epoxy grout and porcelain floor tile are essential. It's the only defensive measure you can take against poor toilet etiquette, by which I mean missing the "target" and leaving a mess on your floor. Unless you already plan to use yellow tile, epoxy grout with porcelain tile is the only way I know to prevent that "yellowing" of the bathroom floor over time.

Area Rugs

When it comes to area rugs, think camouflage. An area rug with pattern and color is your best ally for hiding stains and protecting floors. When you want to redecorate, it's much easier to get a new area rug than it is to restain the wood floor, touch up the tile, or replace wall-to-wall carpeting. You can roll up a soiled area rug, send it out for cleaning, or turn it around to hide an impossible stain under a chair.

For a durable room foundation, start with a colorful, patterned wool rug.

Photo courtesy of Randy Sager

patterned
wool rug--

Photo by Anne Gummerson

Photo by Mark Finkenstaedt

When you shop for synthetic fibers like nylons and acrylics, salespeople will say, "This looks most like wool, feels most like wool." Why not just get wool?

Wool is soft, it's beautiful, and it resists staining. It doesn't mat as readily as synthetic fibers. It's extremely hard wearing and family friendly, and I've yet to hear about any client with allergies having a reaction to a wool rug. I'm not saying that nylon rugs or the new indoor/outdoor rugs made from acrylic and polypropylene shouldn't be used. They should be—mostly in kitchens, family rooms, kids' rooms, or playrooms. They should also be used short-term—until you budget for wool rugs and redecorate.

Photo by Designing Solutions

FLOORS

rugs need patterns and color

Photo by Mark Finkenstaedt

Some rugs last longer than others because of quality, density, color, and wear. I actually think that's a good thing. A lower-priced wool rug will lose its luster and may unravel a bit in a well-trafficked family room, and by the time that happens, it'll be stained, it'll smell, and you'll be ready to replace it anyway. A more expensive, higher-quality wool rug with greater fiber density will outlive you—and it should, given how much you'll pay for it. Wool is a smart fiber—rugs seem to know how long to last and when it's time to be replaced. The quality you pay for will be the deciding factor.

Photo by Designing Solutions

BEFORE

colorful
kid-friendly
rug

AFTER

A flat-weave, reversible rug is a great flooring choice while your kids are young. You can flip the rug over once your kids destroy it, doubling your rug's life span.
Photo by Anne Gummerson

New Zealand wool has the highest concentration of lanolin, which is the same stuff you find in body lotions and hand cream. Not only is wool very soft, but the lanolin provides a natural moisture and stain barrier that causes liquids to bead up. It's like a layer of Vaseline built right into the fiber. But think before you clean your wool rug. If you rub your hands with Vaseline and rinse with water, the Vaseline remains. If you use soap, however, you'll wash the Vaseline right off. With rugs, we want to keep the lanolin. If you spill on a New Zealand wool rug, just blot it with soda water.

Just days after my client's custom-made wool area rug arrived, one of her children was sick ... all over the rug! She was pretty impressed by how easy it was to clean up the mess and remove the odor. That convinced her that New Zealand wool was vomit proof, and we added six more wool rugs to her home!

FLOORS

wall-to-wall carpet

Try running striped wall-to-wall carpet on a diagonal. It makes a small room look more spacious.

Photos by Anne Gummerson

Wall-to-Wall Carpeting

Wall-to-wall carpet adds softness, luxury, and a smooth, continuous surface that, design wise, can't be replicated with area rugs on top of hardwood. Manufactured on broadlooms generally 12 to 15 feet wide, wall-to-wall carpeting is soft and easy on the feet and on your back—you can't slip on it. It provides great sound insulation (you're less likely to hear kids stomping around upstairs while you're downstairs), and wall-to-wall can be less expensive and certainly less messy to install than wood or tile flooring. Wool wall-to-wall carpet is not in everyone's budget, but nylon is, and there are some pretty good choices for truly slob-proof wall-to-wall flooring.

Nylon looks and feels more like wool than ever, but at a much lower price. Older, cheaper nylon can have an artificial-looking sheen, and at the lowest end, nylon can look commercial and feel hard and synthetic. New technology gives higher-end nylon a softer, more natural look, elevating its style and value and resulting in a better-looking product that more closely mimics wool.

The latest-generation nylon, called Tactesse (Stainmaster), really holds up well. It's available in many colors, patterns, textures, and prices, so you can use nylon every-where and get all the durability and cleanability you need without sacrificing style or softness. The exception to this is a family room with a sliding door that opens to a backyard swimming pool. If kids will be tracking in a lot of water with chlorine, go with a solution-dyed acrylic. It can feel a little stiff and it may mat more quickly than other fibers, but nothing can change its color—making it perfect in pool areas.

If you're shopping for wall-to-wall carpet, you can easily get overwhelmed trying to figure out which choice will hold up best for your lifestyle and which fiber offers the best value. Here's a quick primer on the important considerations.

Texture

Texture determines both the surface appearance of your carpet and its resistance to wear and spotting. You'll find four common textures in carpeting:

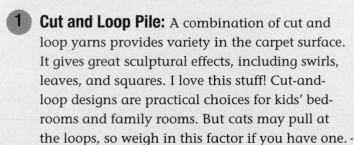 **Cut and Loop Pile:** A combination of cut and loop yarns provides variety in the carpet surface. It gives great sculptural effects, including swirls, leaves, and squares. I love this stuff! Cut-and-loop designs are practical choices for kids' bedrooms and family rooms. But cats may pull at the loops, so weigh in this factor if you have one.

Photo by Fabrica, www.fabrica.com

FLOORS

2 **Multilevel loop pile:** This has two or more different loop heights, to create pattern effects and provide good durability with a more casual look.

Photo by Fabrica, www.fabrica.com

3 **Level Loop:** Looped fibers, commonly called berbers, are all the same height for a consistent, uniform look that offers a casual appearance with great durability. Berbers are popular, hard-wearing choices, but they don't always work well on stairs; with some berbers, the rows of loops can split and expose the carpet backing as the material folds over each tread. Fold a showroom sample over your stairs and make sure you like how it looks.

Photo by Anne Gummerson

4 **Cut pile:** Looped yarns are cut, leaving individual tufts. This is the most popular carpet construction, and the type of fiber, its density, and the amount of twist in the yarn determines its durability. You'll find three basic cut piles:

Plush or *velvet* is a formal, elegant look achieved with a very smooth, uniform surface. Because they show footprints and vacuum marks, the World Floor Covering Association (WFCA) website doesn't recommend plush or velvet textures for high-traffic areas or the rooms of active kids. This is great for an adult bedroom, though.

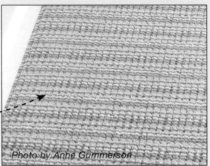

Photo by Fabrica, www.fabrica.com

Saxony is less formal looking than velvet, with yarns twisted so that the ends are visible, though the surface is still smooth and soft. The twist hides footprints. Saxony is popular in living rooms and bedrooms.

Photo by Fabrica, www.fabrica.com

Friezes or *updated shags* have extremely twisted yarns that form a curly, textured surface and give an informal look. The curl minimizes footprints and vacuum marks for a very durable surface. It looks great in contemporary and teen spaces. Friezes are back in style, and they wear like a Mack truck! Each strand in friezes is twisted so tightly that it actually curls over at the end, which allows the carpet to hold its shape better and bounce back after being walked on. But if you're a pet owner and your carpet has fiber strands more than a half-inch long, dander, hair, and dirt can get embedded and be tough to get out.

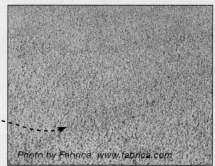

Photo by Fabrica, www.fabrica.com

Density

Density refers to the amount of yarn (usually measured by the inch) in the carpet and the closeness of the yarns. Unlike my husband, who, as we already know, can be pretty dense about wiping dirty feet, the denser the carpet, the better. Nap height measures how high the yarn stands above the backing of the carpet. The shorter the height, the more crush resistant the carpet is, and the better it is for a slob-proof home.

Fibers

Fibers are a carpet's basic ingredient. There are six types:

Olefin or *polypropylene:* A strong stain- and wear-resistant fiber that's easy to clean and resists moisture and mildew. It's suitable for indoor and outdoor installations, but it's not as resistant as nylon to matting and crushing. It's in the lowest price range.

Polyester: Easy to clean and resistant to wear and stains, with a soft feel when used in thick, cut-pile textures. Polyester is not as hard wearing as nylon. It falls into the medium to high price range.

Oy! Neutral flooring! If you must have it, make it the most durable stuff you can buy, like Tact-esse nylon carpet and Dura-Ceramic resilient floor tile.

Photo by Anne Gummerson

neutral slob-proof tile

nylon carpet

FLOORS

AFTER

Photo by Designing Solutions
BEFORE

Acrylic: Moisture and mildew resistant. When solution-dyed, meaning color is added during fiber construction, it's great for homes with chlorine traffic from swimming pools. Acrylic rugs can mat over time.

Nylon: The most popular fiber, with the best stain and wear resistance available. Nylon has excellent softness and the widest color range of the synthetic fibers, and comes in all price ranges.

Wool blends: Wool mixed with nylon provides unbeatable softness, strength, and performance at a lower price than 100 percent wool.

Wool: The fiber by which all others are judged. Soft, thick, and luxurious, wool has great wear performance. However, wool fibers can fade from direct sunlight. Easy to clean, wool is usually the most expensive choice in carpeting.

Padding

Often overlooked in the shopping process, the padding most determines how luxurious your new carpet will feel once it's installed in your home. Upgraded padding makes an inexpensive synthetic carpet feel more luxurious than it really is. Padding helps muffle the sounds of footsteps and acts as a shock absorber, keeping your feet from feeling the hard floor underneath. Most important, good padding can extend the life of your carpet. It protects the carpet backing from friction, which wears it down over time. And padding makes your carpet easier to clean. If your dog Twinkle tinkles in the house, you'll definitely need an antibacterial, waterproof padding under your wall-to-wall carpet. For all these reasons, think of the padding as just as important as your carpet choice.

Carpet Colors

We're thinking camouflage, right? Don't get overwhelmed by all the pretty samples out there—you need a carpet with beauty that's more than skin deep. Ask yourself, "Will this carpet show every speck of dust and every foot impression?" "Will I need to vacuum every day to keep it looking good?" After you've matched the texture, fiber, and density to the room and the people in it, decide on the color.

Bring carpet samples home with you and put them in the worst-case scenarios—at the front door, in the kids' rooms, outside a bathroom, under the doggie bowls, and in the playroom. You want a real-life, actual test drive under extreme conditions before you commit your entire floor or room to a new wall-to-wall carpet. View these carpet choices in your own home, with your room lighting, next to your furniture; the samples will look totally different there than they do in the store.

Getting to the Bottom of Flooring

Here's the bottom line on flooring—the decision process is often like the Scales of Justice. You have to weigh your design preferences and lifestyle against cost, maintenance, and durability. The flooring serves as the foundation of future design decisions in your home, and even the least expensive material, running all through your house, will add up to be a big-budget item. The top priorities for empty nesters

may be beauty and comfort, while a young family on a tight budget may decide their best value is to buy inexpensive, nylon wall-to-wall carpet or resilient flooring that will look good for a few years, and then replace it with wood flooring, wool carpet, and tile when the children are older and the slobs, whoever they are, have left home. Nothing lasts forever—and why would you want it to?

too many rugs

BEFORE

Photo by Designing Solutions

I always think in terms of mixing. Even with a tight budget, you can have a little bit of everything—from the expensive in just a few rooms to the inexpensive, from natural stone and wool rugs to vinyl tile and nylon wall-to-wall. That will stretch your flooring budget and add more luxury and value to your home.

Think of flooring choices like a buffet. You want to take mostly the stuff that's good for you—salad, fish, and a bit of roast beef—but it's hard to resist the desserts, the bread, and those side dishes full of fat and cholesterol. Choose the stuff that's good for you for the high-traffic areas; then, go ahead, live a little—use the less practical stuff in just a few well-chosen areas where your slob rarely goes. Think of marble like chocolate and wool carpet like whipped cream. Just a little goes a long way.

one
big
area rug

AFTER

Instead of using several small rugs on top of a larger, neutral carpet, we used one larger, new rug and matched most of the colors to Riley, the dog, so that shedding hair blends in.

Photo by Mark Finkenstaedt

Shopping List

Nylon Carpet

Fabrica: One of the best-quality synthetic carpet manufacturers in the country. Just a few selections in wool broadloom. Wool area rugs also available. The signature cut velvet in Tactesse nylon, called Chez, is as good as it gets. $$–$$$

Masland: A cousin of Fabrica, has a great selection of synthetic and wool broadloom carpets, some rated for commercial use. Great lines in texture, pattern, and color for every room in the house. $$–$$$

Wool Area Rugs

Company C: Beautiful, hard-wearing wool and cotton area rugs, many with coordinating bedding and toss pillows, in wide selection of colors and patterns. www.companyc.com. $–$$

Sara Schneidman: Very colorful, durable "art" for your floors, hand-knotted and hand-tufted in wool. www.saraschneidman.com. $$$

Safavieh: A collection so vast it'll take you weeks to get through the website. Safavieh has styles for every taste and price range and hard to find sizes, too, with designer collections from Martha Stewart and Thomas O'Brien. www.safavieh.com. $$

Rugs by Vicki Simon: From simple to sublime to spiral, Vicki makes imaginative custom rugs in all colors and sizes. I love her rugs featuring monsters from the deep sea! You gotta love a rug maker with a sense of humor. www.vickisimon.com. $$$

Michaelian Home: Inexpensive, colorful wool rugs and pillows, mostly hooked and country style. Great for "starter" homes and kids' rooms. www.michaelianhome. com. $

Hard Wood Flooring

Natural Cork & More: I use this line over and over again for their hand-scraped, wide plank hardwood flooring. They come "predistressed" so that they hide wear and tear in your home. Styles range from sustainable linoleum, cork, and bamboo to engineered hardwood, oak, and pine. You could do an entire house from this one manufacturer with no two rooms alike. Love it! www.naturalcork.com. $$

FLOORS

Duro Design: Sustainable, durable flooring in planks and square tiles, made from cork, bamboo, oak, and eucalyptus. Softer on the feet than traditional hardwood, but just as tough and in more than 54 colors and graining patterns, Duro Design gives you unlimited design possibilities for creating a unique floorscape. www.durodesign.com. $$

Teragren: Environmentally sound bamboo flooring, countertops, stair risers, and architectural mouldings in beautiful stains and varied plank widths. Their "synergy" line is manufactured and sealed to withstand heavy family use under harsh conditions—perfect for a home full of pets and slobs! www.teragren.com. $$

Resilient Flooring

Fausfloor: If you're choosing a laminated flooring designed to look like wood plank or stone tile, Fausfloor has the market cornered on realism. With so many colors, species, and styles, you'll be easily fooled into believing that it's the real thing, but it's suitable for a basement. www.fausfloor.com. $$

Marmoleum: Ecologically friendly and environmentally sound, Marmoleum offers unique and unlimited colors and patterns in durable flooring. It doesn't try to resemble wood or tile, but instead has its own one-of-a-kind look that's closer to cork. I love the color and pattern possibilities. www.themarmoleumstore.com. $$

Congoleum: DuraCeramic, DuraStone, and DuraPlank are all designed to simulate their "real" counterparts, but with the softness, warmth, and quiet of a resilient floor tile. The most realistic in the line is the DuraCeramic, which comes with or without grout, allowing the tiles to be laid side by side with no gap whatsoever. The simpler the DuraCeramic tile, the better it looks. www.congoleum.com. $–$$

FLOORS

stone tile

natural wood topped with colorful rug

Stone tile in the sunroom and natural wood topped with a colorful, patterned wool rug in the living room provide all the essentials for totally slob-proof flooring.

Photo by Mark Finkenstaedt

Chapter 2
THE BEST SEAT
IN THE HOUSE

I've heard it a hundred times. Shoulders slumped, the clients bring me into their family room and tell me they hate their furniture and need all new seating. The sofa they bought just two years ago is so uncomfortable, no one sits on it. He says she chose it. She says it was all he would let her spend. They both complain that the kids take the pillows off the sofa and use them to lie on the floor, and they need to be cleaned up every morning. The fabric-covered chairs that were brand-spanking-new just six months ago are nothing like the ones they saw in the showroom. Already there are dark marks from hair products on the seat backs and the arms are all worn out because the kids sit on them. "Why do you let them sit on the chair arms?" I ask. "Remember, the sofa is too uncomfortable" they tell me. "We can't afford to keep doing this!" the husband complains. "How do we get it right?"

You know what I'm talking about here. It takes many, many shopping trips, fighting traffic with kids and significant others in tow, to find the right furniture, and then you'll debate for hours over the fabric. Then you wait months for the delivery, stay home all day for the truck to show up at 9:36 P.M., and hope the stuff actually fits in the room. Shopping is stressful, furniture is expensive, and sofas aren't one of those disposable items you can redo year after year.

Photo by Mark Finkenstaedt

padded cushions

What's Underneath the Seat?

Really comfortable, slob-proof upholstery starts with a well-made, well-proportioned frame. If you don't buy for comfort and quality, it won't last. My motto: put your money into the things you sit and stand on. They'll last longer, look better, and still feel good over time, while giving you the best return on your furniture investment. The frame will keep your seating investment looking and feeling good even though your kids bounce all over it day after day, year after year. It's what you don't see— underneath the fabric—that determines a chair's true comfort, durability, and worth.

SEATING

tight seat and
back cushion

indestructible
ultrasuede

Photo by Anne Gummerson

My dad was in the mattress business. He lived and breathed mattresses—it was his life. Wherever we went on a family vacation, the first thing he did was lift the bed covers in the hotel room to see whose mattress we were about to sleep on. He couldn't even walk past a furniture store without going in and posing as a bedding customer, to see whose mattress the salesman would try to sell him first. I remember when he was in the hospital for back surgery. When I saw him in his room after surgery, still groggy from anesthesia, he motioned for me to come close and whispered, "Deb, look under the sheet and tell me what mattress I'm lying on." To speed his recovery, I lied and told him I didn't see a label, but I thought it was his. I knew he'd toss and turn if he knowingly slept on a competitor's mattress. I figured by not knowing for sure, he'd have a reason to get well, get out of bed, and look for himself. And he did!

My dad taught me at an early age to look under the covers (or the cushions), and I always do. Like my dad, you'll sleep better knowing you're on quality stuff. When it comes to seating, here's what you need to know when you lift the cushions.

Three materials are used to make frames—steel, composite wood (essentially engineered wood, with layers of wood laminated together—marketed as a "green" choice), and kiln-dried hardwood (like cherry, mahogany, oak, or maple). Of the three, the most expensive and hard-wearing is the kiln-dried hardwood.

What's underneath really determines a chair's comfort and value.
Photo by Lee Industries, www.leeindustries.com

Photo by Mark Finkenstaedt

sturdy sofa cushion

SEATING

Without getting too technical—after all, this is only furniture—you should expect high-quality seating frames to be made from one of these three materials. Although all three frames are used in good-quality seating, I look for kiln-dried hardwood frames when shopping for myself or for clients. It's just my preference, and it's the way old-fashioned, hand-made upholstery is still manufactured in some U.S. upholstery shops. The process removes any moisture from the wood and leaves it free from possible warping, splitting, shrinking, or swelling—all the things that could happen to wood that isn't dried. The wood is then glued and screwed into a sofa or chair frame, with stress points such as corners and arms reinforced with blocks (a piece of hardwood used to reinforce frame corners) and dowels (pegs that fit into holes to join together the pieces of the frame). The highest-quality frames use double dowels, each measuring about 2 inches long and 1 inch in diameter. Ask "What's in the frame?" when you're in a furniture store. Hardwood, composite wood, or steel with reinforced corners is the minimum you should demand. Don't accept tubing, pressed fiberboard, or plastic.

Steel springs are fitted into frames for support and even weight distribution on the bench—the part where you sit. The most common wire supports are S-shaped sinuous wire frames made of heavy-gauge, tempered steel wire, reinforced with wire ties. Frame supports can also be made from coil-spring wire frames that are individually tied together in eight different directions (back to back, side to side, and diagonally) to provide even greater support, stability, and comfort than the S-shaped wire. This eight-way hand-tied support is more expensive, but both are a sure sign of quality and long-lasting comfort.

Hardwood frames and hand-tied springs make all that good-looking furniture feel good over time.
Photos by Lee Industries, www.leeindustries.com

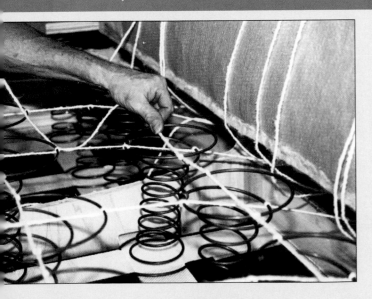
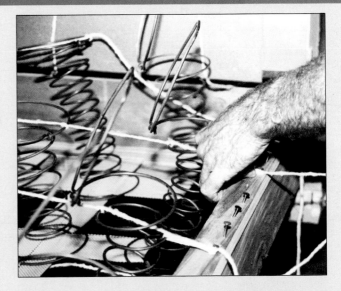

AFTER

There's no excuse for food on the sofa when you have side tables that fold right into the arms!
Photo by Mark Finkenstaedt

attached side tables

SEATING

Even if you don't truly understand what all this means, know that it matters, and ask your salesperson about the frame and springs used to make the upholstery you're about to buy.

If you think of the frame as the skeleton of a sofa or chair, then it makes sense that, without reinforcement and metal springs

BEFORE

Photo by Designing Solutions

(like muscles, cartilage, and tendons), it won't last. Consider the cost of materials and the labor involved in creating a hardwood, kiln-dried, glued, screwed, blocked and doweled, eight-way hand-tied frame, or the equivalent in steel or engineered wood, and you'll instinctively know that a sofa and loveseat advertised on TV or in the newspaper for $999 is crap. Another of my mottos: buy the right thing once, be done with it, and move on. You still need to buy a 60-inch flatscreen high-def TV!

A Cushy Tushie: Cushions

A comfy, durable cushion that will retain its shape over time is critical. Think of Goldilocks: the seat shouldn't feel too hard or too soft, but just right. Additionally, seat cushions should "crown," meaning that they should be plump and have a rising slope in the middle, rather than look flat. Choose—yes, with most upholstery lines you get to choose—your cushion carefully. Most seat and back cushions are made from high-density foam, fiber, feathers, and down, often in combination. The most common and least expensive is the high-density foam cushion, and many manufacturers offer two levels of comfort (and cost) in their foam cushion: standard and premium. Many of my clients find the premium foam very comfortable. It isn't top-of-the-line, but it offers a great "sit" for a small price upgrade. The premium foam's density makes it firmer than the standard, giving your tush better support and making it easier to get up from a sitting position—all factors that matter as you hit middle age!

Whether a dining chair or the family room sofa, choose a well-padded cushion that feels best to you.

crowning cushions

Photo by Designing Solutions

crowning cushions

Photo by Mark Finkenstaedt

The next step up from foam are spring-down cushions, which have coil springs embedded in a block of foam, wrapped in down. This is my favorite choice because the cushions are a bit firmer than even the premium foam, and they maintain their shape well, no matter what happens to them. Made like mattresses, for which I admittedly have an unusual attachment, the spring, foam, and down "bounce" back into shape no matter how many times my kids and their friends bounce on them.

The most expensive cushion is totally down filled, and you don't need it. It's by far the softest and most luxurious choice, but down-filled cushions require constant fluffing and primping after each use, since they flatten out and lose their shape so easily. Down seat cushions can resemble your favorite bed pillow—an old bed pillow—more than a seat cushion unless you're dedicated enough to constantly primp them. I don't like them; they're way too much work. If you want that luxurious, sinking feeling every time you sit down, have a glass of wine, or three, or see if the manufacturer offers a modified down cushion with a foam core, for better shape retention than 100 percent down and more softness than spring-down.

My mom's living room sofa had silk-covered, down-filled cushions. Just thinking about sitting on them left an imprint that, if my sisters and I didn't quickly fluff and primp away, brought my mother's wrath. She was totally nuts about that sofa and those down seat cushions. This can happen to you, too, so beware.

My message here is that cushions are a highly personal thing. Each person reacts differently to seat cushions, often based on his or her height and build. Back cushions, in foam or a foam/down blend, don't come in as many choices. But no matter what you choose for the seat or back, there's no right or wrong. Don't let price play too big a role in determining your choice of cushion fill; the additional cost in upgrading the seat is often minimal and you'll forget about it over the life of the upholstery. It's better to test-drive your upholstery and choose the comfort level that suits you most.

Photo by Randy Sager

Photo by Anne Gummerson

well-padded cushion

CALL YOUR MOTHER— SHE WORRIES!

Once you've made the best choice and the seating is in your home, don't forget to rotate the cushions. You'll extend the life of the seat and back cushions and the fabric covering them. While you're at it, give the cushions and seat bench a good vacuum. You'll probably find the missing Legos and baseball cards that your kids were searching for when they destroyed the rest of the house!

When you shop for new seating, don't forget the padding. It's everywhere—on the arms, on the seat backs, and at the base of the seating. It's usually made from foam, quilted polyester, and dacron. Just pushing down on the arms and back should indicate whether your seating choice has been adequately padded— another surefire sign of quality and lasting comfort. The padding should feel smooth and uniform, not thicker in some areas and thinner in others. You shouldn't be able to feel the underlying frame when you push on the padding. This is another good indicator of whether you're purchasing a piece of upholstery that will last or fall apart once your family gets a hold of it.

Protect Your Seating from Loved Ones: Fabric

My role model, Ida Morgenstern (played by Nancy Walker), knew how to deal with slobs and single men.
Photo©1978 by Ron Grover, courtesy of MPTV.net

Call me Ida. If you're under 40, let me explain … I'm proud to say that many of my slob-proof tricks come from years of watching my favorite TV mom on the old sitcom *Rhoda*. Remember? Rhoda moves away from Minnesota and her best friend, Mary, to go back to New York City and work as a window designer. I once saw myself as Rhoda—young, single, Jewish, and living a stylish, hip life in Washington, D.C. Now I'm old, fat, married with children, and living in the suburbs, just like Ida Morgenstern, Rhoda's mother, who kept all the furniture and lampshades in her Bronx apartment covered in plastic. Armed with just a shopping bag, a dish towel, and a coaster, this little woman knew how to keep her apartment spotless and her furniture protected from family and friends. I use that same Ida mind-set to help protect the furniture in my home and in the homes of my clients— but instead of plastic, I use fabric. Very, very tough fabric. If Ida only knew about stain-resistant, waterproof, antibacterial outdoor fabric!

If you're purchasing new upholstery, you have two options in fabric: You can choose from the fabrics the manufacturer offers or you can find your fabric elsewhere and have it shipped to the manufacturer for use on your seating (known as COM—Customer's Own Material). I almost always choose COM. It gives me infinite choices. I can choose fabric that coordinates with the things my client already has in her home, and I'm not limited to the small offerings from the manufacturer. Other than leather, I rarely find fabrics I would want to use from the manufacturer. Companies just don't have enough colorful heavyweight choices that meet my stringent slob-proof standards. COM is a more

A thick, tightly woven, heavy-duty synthetic fabric makes this sleekly styled chaise totally slob proof!
Photo by Designing Solutions

SEATING

expensive route; the manufacturer doesn't give you much of a price break for *not* using their fabric. And, of course, you'll incur shipping charges when you have the fabric sent to the upholstery factory—but it's the price you pay for getting exactly what you want.

Whether you find something in the furniture showroom or go elsewhere for fabric, or even if you're reupholstering existing seating in your home, the goal is the same as Ida's: you want to cover your chair or sofa with something durable and stain-resistant that will look good and last over time. First, think about the fabric weight. If it's a chintz, polished cotton, or what is known in the business as drapery weight, the fabric will barely last a year, if that. The shiny finish on polished cottons is impossible to live with. Each time you clean a spot, you remove the polished finish. Besides, these lightweight fabrics don't have the thickness to last on everyday upholstery.

chenille fabric covers spots

A thick, checked, prewashed chenille will camouflage spots and still clean up easily with soap and water.
Photo by Mark Finkenstaedt

Now think about the fabric's weave. Hold the fabric, pull it, stretch it, try to look through it. If it's thick and tightly woven, it shouldn't move and should be difficult to see through. Weight and weave are pretty good indicators of how your fabric will perform in real-life situations at home. Additionally, the design industry uses "rub tests" to classify fabrics into categories such as light use, medium use, and heavy use. Not all fabrics are tested, but with slobs in the house, you need fabric that meets the "heavy use" standard, whether it's tested in a laboratory or in your family room. This fabric will endure quite a bit of constant friction and rubbing before showing any noticeable wear.

laminate fabric is easy to clean

If you can't stand the heat in the kitchen, laminate the kitchen chair fabric! The unshiny plastic surface is laminated to the fabric so it wipes clean and feels good.
Photo by Mark Finkenstaedt

Camouflage—Your Best Defense

Once you've tackled weight, weave, and wear, you've got to give careful thought to stain resistance. One Sunday afternoon with my family, for example, and an expensive new sofa could be ruined forever. Color and pattern go a long way toward providing camouflage, and it's remarkable to me that more people don't instinctively choose these fabrics. They choose solids!

Photo by Designing Solutions

BEFORE

So many people email me asking "What color fabric should I choose for my family room furniture?" The answer is right there in front of your face. Choose fabric in the same color as the spots on your existing family room furniture. Look at the color of the spots and stains: if they're mostly red from wine, Hawaiian punch, or tomato sauce, then a new fabric, colorfully patterned with lots of red, will provide good camouflage. After all, if you can't see a spot on your sofa, who cares if you can't clean it out?

Be realistic about your color choices. A white family room sofa just can't stay white in an active household. If you've got a golden retriever who hangs out on the sofa, black fabric doesn't make sense, either. Find a balance between what you really want and what your home really needs. Choose something multicolored, patterned, and easy to clean instead. Save impractical colors like white for small accent pieces that don't get a lot of use or can easily be recovered at a small expense. Choose fabric based on how your family lives now, not how you wish they did.

If you're not up to retraining your dog to stay off the sofa, don't expect it to happen once new furniture is in the house.

In my case, there was no retraining my husband and kids to stop eating messy food on the sofa. Instead, I filled the family room with dark brown leather furniture that I had

What NOT to Wear (on slob-proof seating)

Material	Why?
Polished Cotton	Each time you remove a spot, you remove the polished finish
Light Weight Fabric	It's just not thick enough for everyday use
Loose Weave	Will move, stretch, and become loose and shapeless
Solid Colors	Patterns provide camouflage—not solids

SEATING

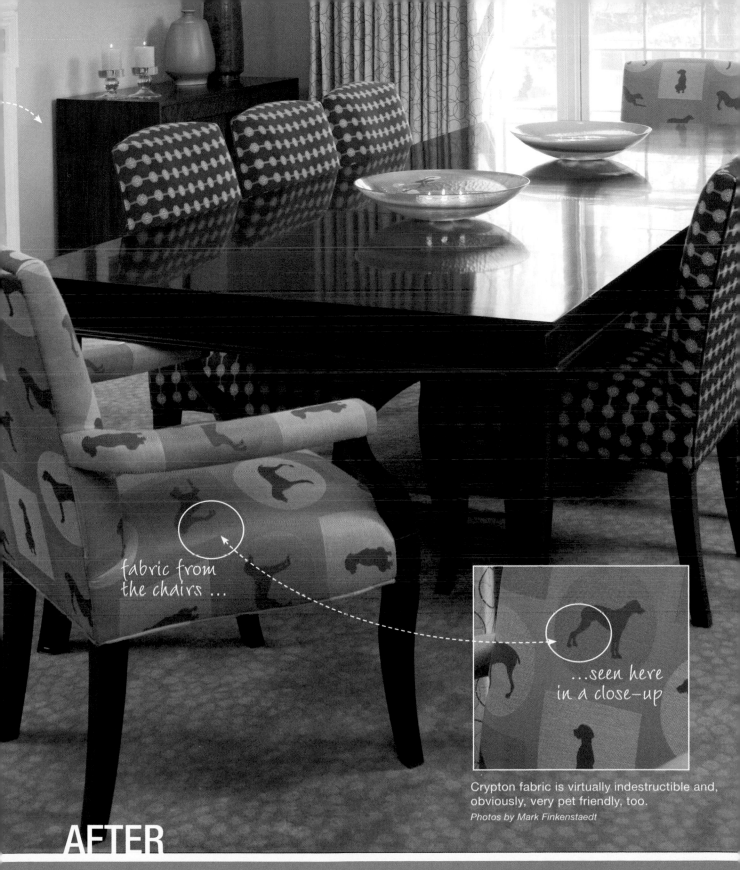

fabric from
the chairs ...

...seen here
in a close-up

Crypton fabric is virtually indestructible and,
obviously, very pet friendly, too.

Photos by Mark Finkenstaedt

AFTER

Sometimes the wrong side up works better. I used the back side of a heavyweight white patterned fabric
to come up with these brown patterned dining chairs.

previously tested at home for stain and scratch resistance. Nothing sticks to it but my husband. One of my clients brought a baggie full of dog hair with her when we went fabric shopping. She wanted to be certain that whatever we used to cover her new sectional would camouflage the dog's incessantly shedding hair. Smart client. She knew what was happening now in her home and expected more of the same. With the bag of dog hair in hand, we made better choices.

Keep your sanity and choose upholstery fabric for the way your family really lives.

SEATING

Photo by Mark Finkenstaedt

Colorful and patterned, this family heirloom is ready for the next generation of slobs.
Photo by Mark Finkenstaedt

And if keeping the fabric clean actually matters to you, choose a cleanable fabric. I don't mean have a spot treatment applied in your home. Those don't last; personally, I think they're a waste of money. Without constant "freshening" and reapplication of the spot treatment, the protection will fail. I mean have a stain barrier built right into the fiber of the fabric rather than sprayed on after the fact. A commercial-grade or outdoor fabric is a better choice; most are truly soil and stain resistant, right down to the fiber level. No coating needs to be periodically applied; the protection is built into the manufacturing process. Most people know outdoor fabric as Sunbrella but, like BandAids and adhesive strips, there are other brands of outdoor solution-dyed acrylic out there, and that's the stuff Sunbrella is made of.

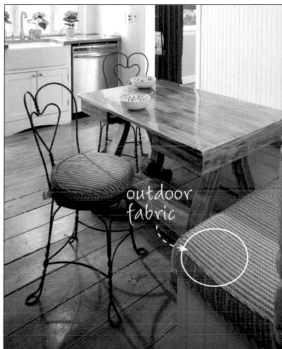

Outdoor fabric is perfect for a kitchen bench and chairs.
Photo by Mark Finkenstaedt

If your husband likes to nap on the sofa, make sure the fabric is soft but thick and durable enough for snoozing and camouflaging smudged newsprint.
Photo by Anne Gummerson

Solution-dyed acrylic is popular because it comes in so many colors, patterns, textures, and price levels—there's something for almost everyone. And it lasts longer than any similar fabric that's not solution-dyed acrylic. In addition to these popular outdoor fabrics, there's ultra- and microsuede (the synthetic alternative to suede) and pleather (a very good-looking synthetic alternative to the not-always-politically-correct leather). Both

Photo by Designing Solutions

BEFORE

ultrasuede and pleather provide great stain resistance and cleanability, come in tons of colors, and are available in varying prices to fit anyone's budget. Bear in mind, though, that fabrics like ultrasuede have a tactile property that makes hair stick to it—so rule it out if your slob has four legs and a tail and/or sheds. It's really tough to remove pet hair and dander from ultrasuede and other fabrics that have similar "sticky" surfaces. You need something smoother, like pleather or the real thing.

stain-proof leather

Soft as butter, but without the cholesterol: scratch-proof, stain-proof leather adds luxury without the worry of it getting ruined.
Photo by Anne Gummerson

SEATING

dog-proof fabric

pet-friendly leather

AFTER

I chose a leather impervious to scratching for a client with a house full of dogs.

The Crypton fabric shown in the close-up above not only has dogs on it, but it's dog-proof and immune to bacteria, staining, and pet accidents.

Photos by Mark Finkenstaedt

SEATING

A word or two about leather: if you have no objections to it, leather makes a great slob-proof choice for seating, if, like everything else, you choose the right one. Remember the clients who hated their uncomfortable family room sofa? It was covered in butter-colored leather, and they hated that, too, complaining that it showed every scratch and spot.

Run your thumbnail down the store leather sample. If you can't see the scratch, the leather meets the first slob-proof test: it won't show marks from claws, cleats, or

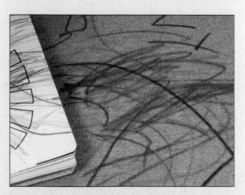

Crypton fabric is truly like Superman—superhuman strength and really good-looking!

Photos by Crypton, Inc., www.cryptonfabric.com

carelessness. Spill a little coffee or soda on it. If you can wipe it off and there's no discoloration left on the leather, it has probably been coated for extra durability. Many manufacturers offer "protected" leathers that have been coated with dyes and/or sealants to make them impervious to soiling and staining. Leather that meets the scratch and spill tests will hold up at home.

If I had to choose one line of fabric to cover every seat in my house, it would be Crypton—a commercial-grade, indestructible fabric that resists spills, stains, mold, mildew, and bacteria. There's even a new line of Crypton leather that performs like the fabric, giving total protection to leather from moisture and staining. I love Crypton fabrics because they come in traditional and contemporary patterns, very fun colors, and off-beat designs while offering virtually worry-free protection for your furniture. A COM fabric from Crypton would make an expensive but indestructible sofa, sectional, or side seat. Imagine using this stuff on dining chairs! You'd probably volunteer to host all the family holidays.

The Details

When I'm sitting at my desk scrolling through page after page of seating selections for clients, I often end up daydreaming of what I would do if I could make my own sofa. I'd start with the great frame and springs I described earlier, with spring-down cushions and, of course, Crypton fabric. But the details would really set my sofas apart from others: exposed legs with indestructible finishes, small rounded arms, generous padding to give great neck support for napping, seat cushions that strap to the sofa base, and back cushions that zip to the back of the sofa. Nothing would move unless I wanted it to—say, for vacuuming purposes. I'd design my sofa with slob-proof styling built right into the details.

Photo by Anne Gummerson

tight back sofa and round arms make a comfortable, slob proof sofa.

Although this sofa is just a dream, you can choose some style details for your new seating right now to make it more slob proof. Did you know that most manufacturers will give you the choice of having a skirt or exposed, finished legs at the bottom of the chair or sofa? You just have to ask! Along with collecting dirt, dust, and shedding pet hair, skirts can get wrinkled and start to flair out. When someone (like my husband or teenage sons) with dirty shoes sits on a skirted sofa, you pay the price with a dirty skirt. I'm not saying that seating with exposed legs is the answer to all your dirty shoe problems, but it does help by fitting any style room and giving a neat, tailored look to any seating. With no skirt, it's one less thing that will get dirty in your home.

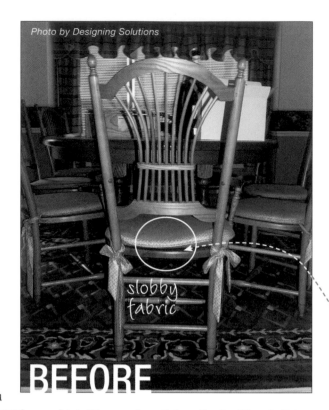

Photo by Designing Solutions

slobby fabric

BEFORE

Seat backs can be styled with large, loose back pillows; multipillow backs layered with smaller back pillows; smooth, upholstered backs with no pillows; and semiattached backs that have large cushion backs attached to the back of the sofa so they can't be moved.

Photo by Designing Solutions

no skirt here

SEATING

stain-proof
chair fabric

AFTER

Dining chairs can get ruined in one night, so I chose a COM fabric that's stain-proof; for a decorative punch, I added a bright green welt in indestructible ultrasuede.

Photo by Mark Finkenstaedt

It's a jungle out there, but an old dining chair bounced back when I covered it in Crypton.

Photo by Anne Gummerson

A chair and ottoman with a standard seat back, no welts, no skirt, and casters has all the slob-proof details to help make your furniture last longer and look better over time.

Photo by Designing Solutions

SEATING

Any Ida out there knows which seat back to choose and which to avoid. Multipillow backs are high maintenance. They not only require constant rearranging and primping to look good and work well, but they are way too tempting a tool for a pillow fight—just avoid them. Upholstered backs with no cushions at all work very well, but some of them lack comfort and that cozy, pillowy feeling that you want when relaxing. Semiattached backs and standard seat backs (one seat-back cushion for every seat cushion, and usually two or three of each) are the most common choices for seating, requiring little primping and fluffing. Standard backs are moveable—you can rotate the seat back cushions to even out wear and tear on the fabric and stuffing. Semiattached cushion backs can't be moved at all but really hold up well in rooms where your kids hang out.

Welts—not the kind on your tush, but the kind on your seat and back cushions—are another style consideration you can change. Welts are fabric-covered cords that get sewn into the seams on the upholstery's edge to firmly define them. They're also quick to stain and wear out. You have the option to choose your welts in a contrast fabric, which adds not only a touch of style to your seating, but also strength. I've done welts in ultrasuede on dining chairs that were covered in fabric. I've used leather welts on wing chairs covered in soft chenille. In addition to looking great and adding a unique style to the seating, the decorative welt adds staying power to an upholstery detail that can be the first area to show signs of wear and tear. It's another layer of protection in the war against your slobs, going on daily in your home.

no arms

no skirt

Slob proofing can be in the details, like small arms, no skirt, and no welt on the cushions to get frayed or stained.
Photo by Designing Solutions

A leather welt on this wing back chair adds style and durability.
Photo by Morgan Howarth

Though not considered a slob-proof consideration, height and pitch are worth mentioning here because they influence comfort—and that's why you're planning to go out test-driving seat cushions in the first place. A sleek, low leather sofa looks fabulous in a furniture showroom, but try watching a football game or movie from this seat, and you'll need a neck brace. By the looks of it, today's low seating choices are more like torture devices than a comfy place to read, nap, or watch a movie. Look through any home design magazine, and you'll see page after page of low, straight-backed sofas with straight, wide arms and sinking seats. After sitting for a while, you'll need a crane to pull yourself out of the ultralow seat. What's up with this?

If you're buying seating for the waiting room of a chiropractor, a low sofa will be good for business. If you plan to watch TV and put your feet up while sitting in a sofa or chair, consider shoulder and neck support essential for your comfort, and rule out

leather welt lasts longer

anything with too low a seat. Sixteen inches or less from the floor is too low; for some, like me, even 17 inches is the minimum height. Don't overlook support for your lower back, either. Any seat or sofa that's too straight will kill your back, especially if you're my age … whatever that is. Pitch, or the angle of the seat and back, is important if you want to really sit in your upholstery. Make sure the seat back supports your lower back.

Check out the arms. A straight tuxedo arm (an arm with right angles) works with both traditional and contemporary rooms, but it doesn't belong in the TV room, where you might want to lie down and rest your head; it's too straight! But a rolled arm is perfect every time. If you don't want your kids sitting on the arms of your sofa, don't choose styles with oversized arms. The arm of the sofa is often the first place where fabric thins out and shows wear. And with abuse, the soft padding under the arm's fabric wears down and the hard frame can be felt right under the fabric. You can't sit on smaller arms, but they do give a little extra seating space on the sofa.

SEATING

spill-proof leather

I couldn't change the neutral carpet, but with a big screen TV on the other side of the room, there was no doubt that the neutral leather seating must be slob-proofed, so it's stain and scratch resistant.
Photo by Designing Solutions

Remember when you were in college living in a dorm? There was probably a TV lounge at the end of the hall where everyone used to hang out. Now imagine that you're about to purchase furniture for that lounge and that it has to last through at least four years of undergraduate school. That's hundreds of parties, pillow fights, spills, and general turmoil as furniture is bounced on, pulled apart, and relocated outside for an entire weekend, in the rain, during Oktoberfest. Armed with my own Ida-style shopping bag full of leather samples, I kept that vision in my head when I looked for new family room seating for my own home. Now, four years later, the sofa I purchased that day still looks and feels good. I followed *Animal House* rules. Ida would be proud.

Shopping List

Fabric/COM

Crypton: www.cryptonfabric.com $–$$$

Ultrasuede: My favorite is Enduraweave, from Leisure Time Marketing. You can't beat the price, weight, or feel. Manufactured for the RV industry, this 100 percent polyester line gets high ratings in every abrasion, colorfastness, flammability, and cleanability test, and is great in both wet (a bathroom vanity stool, for example) and dry locations. Check your local fabric store for availability. $

An ultrasuede sofa with standard seat cushions, small padded arms and exposed legs provides basic slob-proof details.
Photo by Barbara Sweeney

The arm on this sofa is not too big and not too small, but softly rounded for great neck support when you're napping.
Photo by Designing Solutions

Lee Jofa's Crescendo Suede in nylon looks and feels so much like the real thing that you'll have to look at the tag to know the difference. Available in every imaginable color, too. www.leejofa.com. $$$

Groundworks: My "go to" source, time and again, for the unusual; from upholstery fabrics to delicate silks, Groundworks always has something that you haven't seen already coming and going. Through Lee Jofa at www.leejofa.com. $$–$$$

Michael Weiss for Kravet: Kravet is one of the largest fabric houses, and the collection by designer Michael Weiss is worth searching for. His collection includes vibrant colors, bold patterns, and classic geometrics, many in durable, cleanable fibers that will hold up to years of abuse. Mixes well in any style of home. www.kravet.com. $–$$$

Sofas/Chairs/Sleepers

Lee Industries: Don't be fooled by their name. Lee is a family-owned upholstery manufacturer with a broad line of traditional, transitional, and contemporary/country styles to fit most budgets. I use this line more than any other. Quality made from the ground up, Lee offers arm, leg, and cushion options to suit every comfort level and safety precaution. Lee pricing falls in the midrange, and many large chains, such as Crate & Barrel, offer a variety of Lee pieces. www.leeindustries.com. $$

Shaver/Melahn: Sleek and very contemporary, Shaver/Melahn is a high-priced, boutique-style furniture line with firm back support, which is hard to find in contemporary seating. That's why I love it. The line allows you to custom-size your sofa more than most, and the small scale and simple styling make this seating line perfect for small spaces. You provide your own fabric. www.shavermelahn.com. $$$

American Leather/AU Furniture: Made in Texas in about six weeks, American Leather pieces range from traditional to contemporary in durable leathers of every color and price range, including ultrasuede. The line offers chairs, ottomans, loveseats and sofas, recliners, and electronically controlled theater seating. If you're in the market for a sleeper sofa, nothing beats their 24/7 comfort sleeper; it's worth a trip to the store just to check it out. (I own two of them.) On a tight budget? American Leather offers the same quality in a lower- priced line of ultrasuede seating and sleepers called AU Furniture. www.americanleather.com. $–$$$

SEATING

Cisco Brothers: Made in L.A., Cisco offers a wide range of seating styles, from traditional to contemporary, with sustainable wood frames and cushion fills. I love the sleeker, simple styles that fit any size room. Another great seating line made in the U.S.A. www.ciscobrothers.com. $$

My traditional clients couldn't part with their skirts, but were all for durable, heavy weight fabrics in strong color.

Photos by Mark Finkenstaedt

durable fabric and color

durable fabric and color

Photo by Designing Solutions

SEATING

Chapter 3

JUST WINDOW SHOPPING

I've got this one big problem room in my house. It's the "den," where my husband and I hang out to watch our favorite TV shows or read the paper, far from the noise of our kids. It's a problem room because every year I have to redo something. Nothing seems to last more than 12 months in this den (referred to as the library or home office in newer homes). It's not just a money pit—it's a time-consuming problem for me, too.

First it was the sleep sofa. Our den doubles as a guest room, and years ago, a visiting 4-year-old peed on the sofa during a play date. The smell never really came out. But as you know from the last chapter, I switched to protected brown leather and conquered my upholstery dilemma once and for all. Then there were rugs— I'm on my third. The Kilim I started with didn't do well; it was too flat and wrinkled easily

Photo by Designing Solutions

BEFORE

with foot traffic. The next area rug wasn't colorful or dark enough to camouflage all the spilled food and drink spots, so out it went to the garbage. Now we're on the third rug—a colorful, tufted wool rug with lots of brown (in anticipation of baseball cleats full of dried mud) and tomato sauce red. So far, so good.

But the biggest and, by far, most expensive problem in the den has been the window treatments. ("Window treatments" is just a fancy, designer term for the stuff you put on your windows—shades, blinds, draperies, or some sort of curtain.) I started with Roman shades—soft folds of fabric that are made to cover the length and width of the window—in expensive designer fabric that looked beautiful and stayed clean. However, my husband destroyed the string cords you pull on to raise and lower the shades. In custom window shades, the cords need to be handled gently, but with my husband's impatient pulling, the cords knotted and broke. The shades could only stay down. It was time to replace several thousand dollars' worth of window coverings that, once broken, kept the room in perpetual darkness.

Next, I tried full draperies—panels of expensive fabric that flank the sides of each

Window coverings that go up and down fare much better than those that hang on the sides. They're less likely to get dirty.

WINDOWS

AFTER

Window treatments can make a room, just by blocking a bad view, or they can break the room
if they get too much abuse.

Photo by Mark Finkenstaedt

window, from ceiling to floor, and meet to close in the middle. With four big windows, this was not an inexpensive treatment. I was hoping they would last more than a year, but my husband used the curtains as his personal dish towel. Why get up and get a napkin when there's a curtain within easy reach that will absorb pizza grease or wipe up excess salsa? I considered banning him from the den as a long-term solution, but instead I took down the draperies and installed bamboo shades that go up and down. Surrounded by leather and bamboo (neither of which has any absorbent properties), he now uses napkins. He spends his time finding ways to ruin our furnishings, and I spend my time finding ways to outsmart him so the furnishings last. We're quite a match!

WINDOWS

shades that go up ...

Using window shades that go up and out of the way of dog paws helps keep the room looking good longer.

Photo by Mark Finkenstaedt

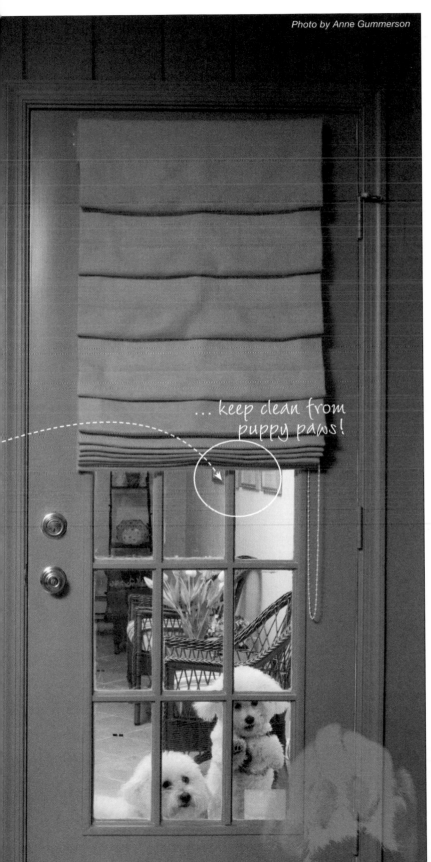

Photo by Anne Gummerson

... keep clean from puppy paws!

I learned through experience that in a house full of slobs, window coverings that go up and down fare much better than those that hang on the sides. They're less likely to get dirty. Curtains that hang to the floor and open and close to the side should be used carefully—in rooms that don't get a lot of use or traffic, like a formal dining room. To open and close full draperies, your slobs will touch and pull on the fabric. Even worse, they could inadvertently step on the hanging drapery, pulling it down from the wall. You wouldn't want these window treatments in the family room or a kids' bedroom unless they're insured. It's better to wait. Once your kids (or your husband) grow up and leave the house, that's the time to get the beautiful draperies you've always dreamed of.

So what do you put on the windows?

You need something; windows shouldn't stay bare, or you'll have no privacy and no light control. Sun exposure can damage rugs, upholstery, and wood floors. Your choices aren't just about covering naked window frames and walls with yards of colorful fabric or keeping light out of your bedroom so you can sleep in on a Sunday morning. Window coverings are an essential component of design and total light management. You can keep your windows simple, with roller shades or fabric Roman shades, or you can

trimming
for style

Simple, but safe from damage, fabric shades are detailed and trimmed for added style.
Photo by Mark Finkenstaedt

mix high-tech gadgetry and slob-proof
durability with the ultimate in automatic
shades and blinds. If you're one of
those who keeps windows permanently
covered with old, warped miniblinds
or still has faded draperies and stained
shades hanging in your revamped
contemporary living room, it's time
to pull them down. Rethink how your
windows and the light coming through
them can enhance the way you live and
work. Privacy, light control, and lasting
good looks are all part of a slob-proof
home's window treatments.

matchstick
blinds

WINDOWS

Matchstick blinds have been around for years but are more popular now as a green alternative for covering windows.

Photos by Mark Finkenstaedt

Defining Window Coverings

Choices abound for surrounding a window with fabrics and trimmings, swags and tiebacks, with names like jabot, empire, and box pleat. But the choices for covering the actual window—the means by which we control light—fall into four basic categories. According to Hunter Douglas, a leading manufacturer I turn to again and again, those categories are as follows:

Hunter Douglas Silhouette Ultraglide window shadings.
Photo used by permission of Hunter Douglas

Roman Cordlock designer screen shades from Hunter Douglas.
Photo used by permission of Hunter Douglas

Window shadings: Shadings combine a soft, sheer fabric with the look of traditional hard blinds, such as the Hunter Douglas Silhouette, Luminette, or Alouette shades.

Shades: Soft window treatments that can be raised or lowered for privacy and light control without sacrificing the view outside. Included are folded fabric shades (Roman shades), pleated fabric, balloon (gathered fabric) shades, roller shades, woven reed and grass or bamboo shades, and honeycomb or cellular types of shades. Some can be custom made from the fabric of your choice.

Which is the best choice for you? Here's the checklist I use:

1. First, consider the style of your home and your own preferences. Do you like strong, simple architectural features or do you prefer something sheer and soft? Are you going for a classic, clubby window look or just the bare basics? Do you want to layer a privacy shade under a soft fabric valance to dress up a room, or keep it simple? Each window shade and blind gives a distinct look and feel to the room; try to choose the covering that best complements your furnishings, room colors, and personal taste.

WINDOWS

Consider the style of your home … and who is using the room … and for what purpose.

Country Woods Reflections Cordlock wood blinds from the Hunter Douglas Collection.
Photo used by permission of Hunter Douglas

Blinds: Considered to be "hard" treatments with veins that tilt or angle to control the amount of light entering a room. They can also be fully "opened" for an unobstructed view. Choices include verticals, horizontals, and miniblinds made from aluminum, wood, or wood alternatives.

Heritance hinged-panel custom shutters from the Hunter Douglas Collection.
Photo used by permission of Hunter Douglas

Shutters: Also a "hard" treatment, shutters are stationary window coverings with moveable vanes for light management, made in wood and wood composite materials.

2 Next, ask yourself who is using the room and for what purpose. A kid's room, a play room, or even a heavy-use family room needs a more durable window covering that's up to the challenge of messy hands or, if operated manually, heavy cord pulling. This is a perfect place for a remote-controlled shade or blind. A seldom-used living room can take a window covering that requires gentle primping to look its best, like a soft-fold Roman or balloon shade made in the fabric of your choice. Even a floor-to-ceiling drapery can work in rarely used rooms or when it's hanging behind furniture so there's little access to it, limiting the possibility of damage.

WINDOWS

This roman shade perfectly complements the room's style and furnishings.

Photo by Mark Finkenstaedt

This heavy-duty bamboo shade minimizes aggravation and gives good light control. It's a good-looking green choice that fits any décor.

Photo by Designing Solutions

3 Know your light control and privacy needs. Is the room dark or bright? Do you need privacy from neighbors or the street outside? Will sunlight coming through the window damage your furnishings or put a glare on your TV? The amount of privacy and light control you need in each room is an important factor in choosing the right covering for your windows. Some coverings will never give you full blackout, and others may never let in enough light.

4 Finally, how much aggravation can you tolerate? I personally have had a heck of a time trying to get minimicro Star Wars action figures out of the 2-inch horizontal veins in my Silhouette shade. (When they were younger, my kids stuck them in my 42-inch-wide shade.) I had to take down the shade and shake it to get the toys lodged out of the middle. If I had to do it over, I would have used a roller shade. I have also found that 2-inch wooden blinds on doors get dented easily by swinging backpacks or just by slamming the door.

Most homes have an assortment of window treatments. One of my clients has three rambunctious shedding dogs and has one of every type of window treatment in her home. The dogs aren't allowed in the master bedroom, so we splurged on silk draperies, with blackout linings, so the room is dark when the window is fully covered. In the TV room, we used woven reed and grass blinds that fold up to the top of the window and come down just to the sill. Their glossy finish allows my client to dust and wipe them without any fear of damage to the shade. For kids' rooms, we added accordion-style shades on remote, so the shade itself is never touched by human hands. Knowing exactly what light control you need, what style you're going for (contemporary or traditional, soft and cozy, or simple and sheer), and who or what is in the room helps you zero in on the best choices. And since most houses come with a minimum of 20 windows (some have close to a hundred!), you'll want to mix it up without making a costly mistake.

Sometimes less is more. If you don't need to cover the windows but just want to give them a finished look, a simple fabric valence is the perfect solution.
Photo by Anne Gummerson

simple fabric valence!

woven grass shade

A sturdy woven grass shade shimmers in the afternoon sun.
Photo by Mark Finkenstaedt

Window Panels: The Exception to the Up-and-Down Rule

Although my experience as a mom, wife, and designer tells me that, for sanity's sake, you should stick to window coverings that go up and down rather than side to side, I have to tell you about window panels. They're new to the market, and these coverings can make a hardy alternative for large-scales windows where none of the coverings described above will really do the job. Tracks are attached to the ceiling—just as in a standard vertical track system of the 1970s, but the panels

Photo by Designing Solutions

heavy wood shade

BEFORE

WINDOWS

soft colorful shade

AFTER

The best solution here was to replace a hard shade (the wooden blind) with something soft and full of color.

Photo by Morgan Howarth

window panels

window panels

Hunter Douglas Skyline window panels.
Photos used by permission of Hunter Douglas

WINDOWS

are made of every fabric and fiber imaginable and in any width, instead of the hard 3- to 6-inch synthetic strip currently used in vertical blinds. A typical individual panel width can range from 12 to 40 inches. The quantity of panels depends on the width of the window opening and the desired effect. More overlapping panels give a layered, opaque look, while abutting panels offer a more contemporary, airy look.

Window panels are versatile because they can be matched identically to other fabrics being used in your room. Panels made with solar screen fabric will keep out heat and damaging UV rays but still allow an unobstructed view. Use a slob-proof fabric on a window panel, and you've got a unique, vertical window covering that will hold up to your family.

Yes, window coverings that go up and down are still my preference, but sometimes adding blind after blind to a room full of multiple sliding doors or windows just doesn't make sense. Combined with durable, cleanable fabric, panels are the next best thing.

Going Topless

Tell your husband or partner that you're thinking of going topless, and you'll immediately capture his attention … that is, until he finds out you're talking about window treatments. Bottom-up/top-down shades allow you to cover just the bottom of the window—where privacy is truly an issue—while leaving the top part of the window open to allow natural light or fresh air to enter a room. This option works well in bedrooms, bathrooms, home offices, and dining areas, especially if these rooms face a street or a neighbor's house.

In most cases, you have the choice, since most window coverings can be made to do this: to close the shade from the top down, as in traditional window coverings; to close it from the bottom up; or to close it from either the top or the bottom. You have total control over light, view, and privacy, and can leave the top, bottom, or some point in between fully closed or open to the outside world. The only drawback—to function, this shade has two entirely different sets of cords instead of one, with each cord working in one direction, either to pull the shade up or to pull it down. It's simple to operate, but when the shade is fully dropped down to the window sill, the cords show. It's no big deal to me, and I love the combination of privacy and daylight. But the exposed strings are another place where dust can collect and kids can pull on the cords.

bottom-up shade

If you keep those darn strings clean, a bottom-up shade gives just the right amount of privacy and light.
Photo by Mark Finkenstaedt

Wiring Your Windows

More than other home fashions, window styles have changed to meet new consumer demands, child safety regulations, and home design trends. Are you old enough to remember the introduction of vertical blinds and how their popularity grew in the 1970s as builders incorporated sliding glass doors into their new homes? Now, more than 30 years later, it seems that you can't buy a new house that doesn't have an inaccessible second-story window in the foyer or great room. And once again, the window treatment business has responded with battery-powered and hard-wired electronic features for window products. Almost any window covering you can think of can come with hands-free operation at the touch of a button. The convenience comes with a premium price tag, increasing the cost of some window coverings by as much as 150 percent, but for many of us, the additional cost is well worth the convenience, control, and peace of mind.

remote-controlled
window shade

The only downside I can see in using remotes is that the kids are likely to lose them.
But once they clean up their piles of dirty
laundry and books … whew, there it is!

Photo by Mark Finkenstaedt

Your options include battery-powered, hand-held remote controls and timers that raise and lower windows at preset hours. Some sunshades can adjust automatically as sunlight hits your windows, lowering inch by inch as the sun moves! By eliminating manual controls—like cords and wands—windows stay cleaner and free from damage. For a homeowner with limited mobility or slobs with sticky fingers, these power options are ideal. They're safer around small children, too (no strings or cords to get tangled up in).

Another benefit of automated shades that makes the increased cost a little easier to swallow is that the shade operation can be linked to your home theater controls or security system. When they're linked to a home theater system, you can control unwanted light during movie viewing; when the theater is activated, the shades will close automatically. As part of a home security system, shades can go up in the morning and down in the evening—automatically—to give your home a secure, lived-in look.

Battery-Operated Window Coverings

I'm a big fan of remote-controlled window treatments. I recommend them in almost every design job I do. They're affordable and they help make your shades last longer. Besides, our kids have grown up on remote controls—for TV, gaming systems, ceiling fans. Everything has a remote! Your kids will use them. So consider them for every room in the house. (One caveat—remotes won't work on shades that are layered underneath fabric valances or draperies. You have to aim the remote at the exposed head rail.)

I am a big fan of remote controlled window treatments. I recommend them in almost every design job I do.

WINDOWS

battery-operated windows

Can you imagine your kid opening and closing all these window blinds by hand?
Photo by Mark Finkenstaedt

Automation not only lifts and lowers window coverings, but it can also tilt blinds with slats and vertical shades. There's no wiring connected to an electrical supply—just batteries controlling a motor hidden in the headrail. So no electrician is involved. Bear in mind, though, that batteries have power limitations and may not be suitable for oversize windows that need greater "pulling" power to move up and down.

If changing batteries and losing remotes is too much of a hassle, hard-wired window coverings may be the perfect choice.

Hard-Wired Window Coverings

If changing batteries and losing remotes is too much of a hassle, hard-wired window coverings may be the perfect choice. Additionally, if you've chosen a heavy window covering or blind, or if you have oversize windows, hardwiring may be your only option when it comes to providing sufficient "pulling" power. Hard-wired shades are controlled like any other built-in electrical appliance in your home. Some come with a choice of a battery-operated, hand-held remote or a wall switch—or both. It's like using a television—you connect the TV to the household electrical system and control the TV with both a remote and an on/off switch on the television set itself.

If you're considering motorizing your shades and blinds and cost isn't an issue, hire a designer to help you make the right choice and order the right size. For hard-wired coverings, you should also consult an electrician before ordering.

Tailored for a teen, these soft-fold roman shades are trimmed with beads and dragonflies.
Photo by Mark Finkenstaedt

No matter what you're choosing for your windows, consulting with experts makes perfect sense. If you're unsure of what colors to use, if you're confused about whether to use an inside or an outside mount, or if you have problem windows that you can't reach and measure for yourself, make it somebody else's problem! Since most fabric shades, like Roman or balloon shades, are custom made to fit the size of the window, it makes perfect sense to work with a pro to help find the perfect fabric and get the shade made and installed correctly

WINDOWS

for you. The extra cost of working with a designer or window expert is more than worth the extra cost of making mistakes on your own.

café-style curtains

"Café-style" curtains will stay cleaner than draperies because they are off the floor.
Photo by Mark Finkenstaedt

Often the safest place for draperies that hang to the floor is the master bedroom. For my client who loves dogs but doesn't allow them in her bedroom, we used dog-head finials.

Photos by Mark Finkenstaedt

WINDOWS

floor length drapes

dog-head finial

Shopping List

Carol's Roman Shades: I love all the ways Carol's Roman Shades makes a simple fabric shade look extraordinary. They offer a large selection of their own fabrics and trimmings, or they'll make their shades with yours. They work with window professionals and designers, so ask them for a referral in your area. Full of beautiful pictures and detailed descriptions, their website is a great guide for choosing fabric shades for your own home. www.carolsromanshades.com. $$–$$$

Hunter Douglas: The leader and innovator in the shade and blind industry—no other manufacturer offers such a variety of window products, with so many quality details. From shutters to sunshades, battery remote to hard-wired wall switches, to manual lift mechanisms with child safety features, Hunter Douglas has it all, and no one does it better. Every reputable window covering store carries this line. www.hunterdouglas.com. $$–$$$

Conrad: You can find matchstick and bamboo blinds everywhere, but they're not like these. Conrad shades offer impeccable styling and quality. Their earthy, organic-feeling fibers, fabrics, and weaves are one-of-a-kind and can't be found elsewhere. www.conradshades.com. $$$

A valance is often the perfect solution for adding color, softness and a finished look to windows.
Photo by Mark Finkenstaedt

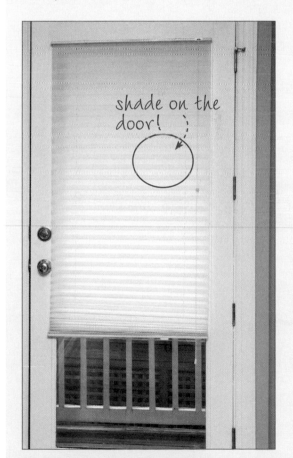

Shades on the door? Sure—you can have the view when you want it and privacy when you need it.
Photo by Anne Gummerson

Boa trim on the bottom of this billowy fabric shade makes it perfectly styled for a young lady's room.

Photo by Anne Gummerson

boa-trimmed valance

WINDOWS

Oy Vay, a neutral room! But the client chose window treatments wisely, knowing that less would be more.

Photo by Designing Solutions

Save the silk and the drapery style for "safe" rooms- like this very adult master bedroom.

Photo by Mark Finkenstaedt

silk drapery is for adult rooms

WINDOWS

valance

A soft and pretty valance tops off the harder woven grass shades underneath.

Photo by Randy Sager

dressy fabric is off the floor

An Austrian shade full and colorful makes a great choice for dining rooms in homes with dogs.

Photo by Designing Solutions

Photo by Barbara Sweeney

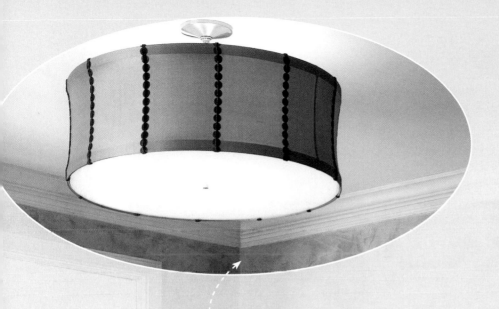

Chapter 4

LET THERE BE LIGHTING

If I've learned anything in my years as a designer, it's this: nothing affects how you feel in your home more than the lighting. Good lighting makes even the most modest rooms look impressive. Without great lighting, even impressive rooms and furnishings look modest. Don't underestimate the power of good lighting. Without it, it's almost impossible to add color without darkening a room.

A large drum-shaped pendant (or a single hanging fixture) adds light, fills empty space between the low bed and tall ceiling and keeps table tops clear.

Photo by Anne Gummerson

Ask any photographer: the additional photography lighting the pros use makes interior room shots and portraits look good. Even if your present budget doesn't allow for any new fixtures, upgrade your bulbs to their maximum wattage or, better yet, to full-spectrum fluorescent or LED bulbs. Replace recessed flood lights with brighter, whiter halogen flood lights. Make what you have do a better job without the expense of hiring an electrician.

drum-shaped pendant light

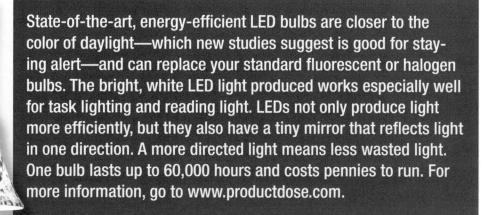

State-of-the-art, energy-efficient LED bulbs are closer to the color of daylight—which new studies suggest is good for staying alert—and can replace your standard fluorescent or halogen bulbs. The bright, white LED light produced works especially well for task lighting and reading light. LEDs not only produce light more efficiently, but they also have a tiny mirror that reflects light in one direction. A more directed light means less wasted light. One bulb lasts up to 60,000 hours and costs pennies to run. For more information, go to www.productdose.com.

LIGHTING

fixture is focal point

A decorative hanging fixture over a table must provide adequate illumination *and* be a design focal point, so I always go bigger.

Photo by Stacy Zarin

If you have the money to spend on lighting, don't skimp. Allow for separate and distinct types in each room to support what you do and what you want to see, whether it's reading or peeling vegetables or, after 19 years of marriage like me, contemplating your wedding photos on the wall.

Lighting Zones

When I'm designing a home, I use three different kinds of lighting: ambient, for overall room illumination; task, located at work spaces such as kitchen counters, desks, make-up areas, and closets; and art, for showcasing architectural features, wall art, and tabletop displays. I divide these three types of lighting into zones, each with its own distinct fixture style and switch. This way, I can choose to light up just the room's artwork or fireplace, a reading area, or even a kitchen counter where I've laid out coffee and dessert in an otherwise dirty kitchen. More than just illumination, the right lighting helps focus attention away from architectural flaws or areas in a room that you don't want to see.

Thinking through how you will use each room, where you're placing furniture and what visual things you want to focus on will lead you to the correct lighting.

Ceiling fixtures provide more than just light— they're eye candy, too.

Photo by Anne Gummerson

ceiling fixtures can be fun!

LIGHTING

hockey
puck–style lighting

Even in my own little master bedroom—a mere 14'×16'—I have all three different types of lighting, each with its own dimmer switch. But before I purchased or installed anything, I gave a lot of thought to how I wanted the room to look, feel, and function. I examined how much natural light was in the room during the day. I thought through where clothing would be placed, where artwork would hang, and how much light we would need for reading in bed, both during the day (which happens only on Sunday mornings, with the papers) and at night. Thinking through how you'll use each room, where you'll place furniture, and what things you want to focus on visually will lead you to the correct lighting.

Versatile hockey puck–style lights can go anywhere and light up anything, like this brick wall and glass-topped table.
Photo by Mark Finkenstaedt

LIGHTING

recessed lighting

art lights

I used three different lighting zones in this hall: tracks of Christmas tree–style lighting in the cutaway ceiling for ambient lighting, recessed lighting to punch up the architectural details in the doorway, and low-voltage art lights to show off the clients' collection of glass art in the two side display towers. With all the light focused at eye level and above, the clients won't ever notice dirt on the floor!

Photo by Mark Finkenstaedt

Most contractors don't give you any choice and install recessed lights like two airport runways in the ceiling. It's better to plan where your furniture will be placed and have recessed lighting installed where you'll need the light—in front of storage cabinets you'll be opening, centered over counters and desks, and especially in dark corners where you might want to display something on the wall.

Ambient Lighting

The first type of lighting to think about is ambient, overall room lighting, which usually comes from ceiling fixtures, multiple wall sconces, and table lamps. Some homes come with a ceiling fixture centered in every room; others have nothing. My rule of thumb in choosing ambient lighting is to keep as much of it as possible in the ceiling or on the walls and as little as possible on tabletops and floors. It's simple preservation. There's less chance of someone throwing a Nerf football at your recessed lights or ceiling fixture, but a very good chance that wall sconces or table lamps placed near seating will get knocked around.

odd number provides symmetry

If you're using a group of small hanging fixtures over a long table, remember that odd numbers provide symmetry and look better.

Photos by Mark Finkenstaedt

rectangular fixture
for long tables

LIGHTING

AFTER

Photo by Mark Finkenstaedt

My problem with most dining rooms is that a round centered fixture lights up only the very center of a long, rectangular table, so consider something linear like this to better light up the entire length of the table.

Photo by Designing Solutions

BEFORE

Of course, just weeks after installing wall-mounted art lights behind my family room sofa, my kids broke one with a misfired Nerf ball. I know what you're thinking and you're wrong—they're not bad kids. They were watching a football game and were overcome by an insatiable urge to throw a ball—and who can blame them? When I watch the Food Network, I'm overcome by an insatiable urge to eat. Anyhow, it took three weeks for the broken parts to come in and then another two weeks to get my electrician back to fix it. Ambient lighting, safely located in or on the ceiling, will provide enough room illumination to make the room usable. My personal preference is recessed lighting; if you install a lot of it, your room won't be just usable—it'll be functional.

Recessed Lighting

If you're choosing recessed fixtures for overall lighting, select those that adjust in your ceiling. Although these adjustable recessed lights are more expensive than the nonadjustable down lights we're all used to seeing, adjustable lights offer greater flexibility. Recessed lights are permanent, but you may change your furniture or art display. Adjustable recessed lights allow you to better aim the light just where you want it, when you want it, up to 40°.

When it comes to the size of recessed lighting, choose the smallest possible aperture for the job. Although the low-voltage lights I refer to as "art" lights come small, line-voltage recessed lights used for overall ambient lighting come in three basic sizes—6¾ inch, 5 inch, and 3¾ inch. In most 8-foot-tall rooms, the standard 6¾-inch recessed light opening is too big. With several of them in your ceiling, you get a Swiss cheese effect: many large holes. Unfortunately, this is the trim size most contractors use. Opt instead for a 5-inch aperture in a room with a standard ceiling height. Use a 3¾-inch light for small spaces—several of them, installed about three feet apart, work perfectly in a narrow hall. The only rooms that can really take the larger 6¾ openings are those with ceilings taller than 8 feet.

LIGHTING

pendant lights look nice over tables

AFTER

A series of small, individual hanging fixtures (pendants) spaced out over a long table also does a great job of lighting up both ends of the dining area.

Photo by Mark Finkenstaedt

Today's choices in recessed lighting include smaller apertures, slots, and pinholes that focus narrow beams of light, and finishes to match every décor, like these in stainless steel. Their narrow beams of light focus on the things you really want to see and away from the things you don't—like a messy area in the room or the dust on the glass-topped table.

Photo by Anne Gummerson

Ceiling Fixtures

Decorative ceiling fixtures, the kind that mount directly *on* the ceiling, should hang no more than 10 to 12 inches for an 8-foot-tall room. For taller rooms, you can choose a fixture with a close-to-ceiling mount that hangs a little lower—12 to 18 inches. How much the fixture should drop depends on the height of the room's ceiling.

If you've got tall people in your home, give thought to head clearance. My husband is 6 feet, 6 inches tall. He can't even clear door openings without bending. As a result, I don't use ceiling fixtures in my home for ambient lighting. I use recessed lights, and I truly believe they have saved my husband several trips to the ER.

BEFORE

Photo by Designing Solutions

LIGHTING

silk in shade

silk in shade

Adding hand-painted silk in this slob-proof home wasn't an option, unless we put it on the ceiling as a decorative fixture.

Photo by Mark Finkenstaedt

Out of harm's way, a gorgeous silk fabric covers this custom light fixture and makes the foyer.

Photo by Mark Finkenstaedt

Task Lighting

The second type of lighting I use, task lighting, is critical for work, study, and recreation spaces. Task lighting makes a room multifunctional. You have to be able to see what you're doing! Don't you just hate going into a powder or ladies' room that's so dim and dark, it's impossible to touch up your lipstick or see if you spilled something on the front of your blouse? The same requirements apply at home. You need adequate lighting over cook and prep areas in the kitchen, in a home office, and especially in areas where you read or where your kids do their homework. Usually overlooked, I also add really good fluorescent lighting in closets so my family can tell the difference between navy blue and black—as if they care! (Fluorescent lighting is perfect for closets and any small, closed-in spaces because it doesn't give off any heat.)

Single light hanging fixtures—like these glass pendants—provide great task lighting over work and cooking areas.
Photo by Randy Sager

It's easy to add reading lamps that bend or have extending arms and pivoting shades on a desk or by a bed. The light needs to reach you. You can also use wall sconces by a bed, with moveable arms and tilting heads, so that you can aim the light just where you need it. Over a kitchen counter or a desk that's placed in the middle of a room, you have to rely on fixtures that are installed in or on the ceiling.

Anything that gives off bright, focused light just where you need it will do the job, including recessed lighting, track lighting, pendant fixtures that suspend from the ceiling, wall sconces, and occasional adjustable table and floor lamps. For task lighting over the bed, a desk, or kitchen counters, you want the light installed in front of where you'll be standing or lying down, not behind. Why? When recessed lighting is behind you, your body casts a shadow on the very surface you're trying to light up. Find the spot where you normally lay your head on your bed pillow, and install a recessed light for reading right above it. In kitchens, install recessed lighting so that it's centered over a kitchen island.

Wall sconces framing a mirror give great make-up light. If anything's amiss, you'll see it.
Photo by Mark Finkenstaedt

LIGHTING

single
light fixtures

Photo by Designing Solutions

Go with what fits your style, lifestyle, and budget. I used two types by my bed for reading. First, I placed two small, low-voltage recessed lights, one over my pillow with its own dimmer switch, and one over my husband's. I also added two bendable, adjustable desk lamps in chrome, just like the animated type that appears at the

start of Pixar films, one on each side of the bed. The arm extends and pivots 360°
from its base, and the bendable shade houses a little halogen bulb. It's perfect for
lighting up a bedside chest and the insides of its overstuffed drawers. With separate
lights and controls, I can nod off to sleep in relative darkness while my husband reads.

Lamps

Beware of lamps with fabric
shades. They don't do the job as
well as lighting mounted on or in
your ceiling. Besides, the shades
are always hanging crooked, and
then you have the electrical cord
(and sometimes even an extension
cord) to conceal. Instead, choose
decorative ceiling fixtures and
sconces that complement the
room's style and design and keep
lighting off tabletops wherever
possible. In my little master
bedroom, for example, I chose a
ceiling fan with a flat, unobtrusive
integral light to use for ambient
lighting. It's often the first light I
turn on when I walk into the dark
bedroom.

Art Lighting

My favorite lighting—art
lighting (at least, that's what
I call it)—showcases wall and
tabletop displays and a home's
architectural features. You can
use it anywhere: to spotlight a
painting over the fireplace, a set
of photographs on a stair wall, or
a piece of pottery on a coffee table.
You also can use it to highlight an

monorail art lighting

How do you light up artwork going up and down the stairs? A
curvy low-voltage monorail does the trick better than anything
else.

Photo by Anne Gummerson

interesting corner or column, tile, or stone wall. Art lighting can be recessed in your ceiling, mounted as a wall sconce, or installed as track lighting. I use small 3¾-inch low-voltage lights that give off a bright, white burst of concentrated light, just as you would find in an art gallery or museum. To me, this art lighting sets the mood and "makes" the room, letting you focus attention on the things you love and away from the things you don't want to see. Used correctly, art lighting can camouflage torn furniture, stained walls, even damaged flooring just by focusing all that bright light on the few good pieces in the room.

I added two kinds of art lights in my little bedroom. First, around the room's perimeter, I used 3¾-inch low-voltage recessed lights to showcase anything hanging on the walls. I skipped the wall space where we placed a TV; you don't want to add any glare on TV screens. I measured the distance from the center of the wall hanging to the ceiling and divided that measurement by half. That's how far from the wall I had the recessed art lights installed in the ceiling, and it's a good *general* guideline for most recessed light placement. These recessed lights are on their own dimmer switch.

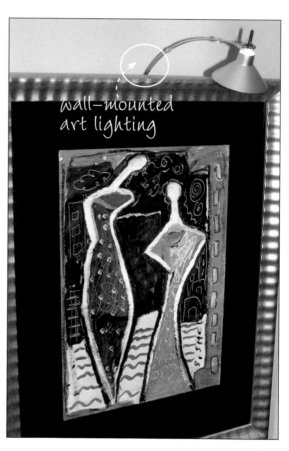

If I had it to do over again, I wouldn't have used wall-mounted art lights in my own family room—too many flying Nerf balls for my peace of mind.

Photo by Designing Solutions

Monopoints

I also added itsy-bitsy track-style monopoint lights. They're not recessed; they're little flashlight-looking bulbs on stems—about 3 inches in length—that are installed *on* your ceiling rather than *in* your ceiling. They swivel on their stems 360° for maximum aiming, and I have five of them focused on some pottery sitting on the top of a tall wardrobe. Installed on the ceiling in front of this storage piece, the lights also illuminate the clothes inside the tall wardrobe when we open the doors. At night, I can turn on the dimmer switch that controls just these lights, and the pottery—all of it jugs with ugly faces—lights up and makes me smile. Recently, my husband and kids covered each jug with a baseball hat, and now they like to turn on the lights at night and see all their favorite team logos light up. It's a conversation piece that wouldn't work without the high-impact art lighting.

Photo by Mark Finkenstaedt

Photo by Designing Solutions

The under-rated monopoint is so versatile, shedding light anywhere you need it, with 360° of aim.

Controlling the Light

Once you've gone through the trouble and expense of setting up three lighting zones for yourself, you need to be able to control them separately from one another. One switch won't do. When I'm doing a client's lighting, I always add new dimmer switches, new receptacles (the real name for "plugs") to match, and new screwless plates.

Put every lighting zone on its own dimmer. Dimming your lights saves energy and money, extending the life of the light bulbs and allowing the dimmer to pay for itself in a very short amount of time. And separate dimmers give you control over the room's lighting. You can set the mood, control which features are highlighted, and change the look and feel of the space. But best of all, when you upgrade your dimmer switches and receptacles, you can switch your old plates for new, screwless plates in scrubbable, matte finishes. You won't see any screws holding these plates to the wall, peeling or chipping paint around the screws, or dirt to clean. The new screwless plates always look better, show fewer fingerprints, and come in so many

When you upgrade your dimmer switches and receptacles, you can switch your old plates for new, screwless plates in scrubbable matte finishes. Why care? You won't see any screws holding these plates to the wall—no peeling or chipping paint around the screws, no dirt to clean!

colors, you can coordinate them with paint and trim or choose a cool, translucent seafoam green to stand out against the wall. New Diva dimmers from Lutron, a top manufacturer of lighting supplies, have large touch pads and come with a pale orange backlight, allowing you to see the wall switch in the dark. They're my favorite choice.

Photo by Mark Finkenstaedt

screwless plates

Photo by Mark Finkenstaedt

LIGHTING

remote-controlled
lighting

Remote-controlled lighting? I got tired of hearing, "Mom, can you turn out the lights?" When your kids are done reading and are ready to drift off to sleep, empower them to turn off the lights from bed, by themselves.
Photo by Mark Finkenstaedt

The best-lit rooms and homes have multiple lighting zones and combinations of recessed lights, decorative fixtures, and ceiling-mounted fixtures. This gives you maximum lighting possibilities and adds visual interest to your home. A typical living room, for example, looks great with a large decorative ceiling fixture centered in the room and recessed lighting around the room perimeter to highlight bookcases and art, and to light up dark corners. Think mix!

A typical room needs more than one kind of lighting. Here, the focal point is the hanging fixture, which is great for lighting up the table. But little, low-voltage recessed lights in stainless steel do the job of lighting up the room's perimeter.

LIGHTING

hanging fixtures

recessed lighting

Photo by Mark Finkenstaedt

stagger hanging pendants

I had to use four pendants over this table to provide adequate lighting, so I staggered the length of the hanging cords for a far more interesting look.

Photo by Barbara Sweeney

Shopping List

Decorative Ceiling Fixtures

Stonegate Lighting: Fabulous fixtures and lamps, ranging from fabric-covered drum shade pendants to art glass. Lots of fabric choices. *www.stonegatedesigns.com.* $$–$$$

Arroyo Lighting: From Arts & Craft to rustic country, coordinating ceiling fixtures, hanging fixtures, sconces, and exterior lights in great finish choices and multiple glass finishes. *www.arroyo-craftsman.com.* $$

upgrade outdoor fixtures

Stylish and practical, upgrade your outdoor light fixtures to better complement the lighting inside your home.
Photo by Mark Finkenstaedt

Seascape Lighting: Contemporary fabric-covered hanging fixtures and table lamps on a budget. www.seascapelamps.com. $

Forecast Lighting: Pendants, ceiling fixtures, and wall sconces that give a lot of bang for the buck. With something for every budget and style, it's my old faithful. www.forecastltg.com. $–$$

Estiluz: Contemporary, classy halogen and fluorescent ceiling fixtures. www.estiluz.com. $$$

Art Glass Pendants

Oggetti: Colorful glass fixtures from Italy that you won't see coming and going. www.oggetti.com. $$–$$$

2 Thousand Degrees: Readily available glass pendants in every shape and color. www.2thousanddegrees.com. $$

LBL: Glass pendants and cool-looking wall scones, monopoints, and ceiling fixtures in glass. www.lbllighting.com. $$

LIGHTING

Recessed Lighting

Lightolier: Line- and low-voltage recessed fixtures for every application and price range. The industry standard. www.lightolier.com. $–$$$

Halo Iris: Line- and low-voltage recessed lighting in unique trim colors and shapes— even square. www.iris-lighting.com. $$–$$$

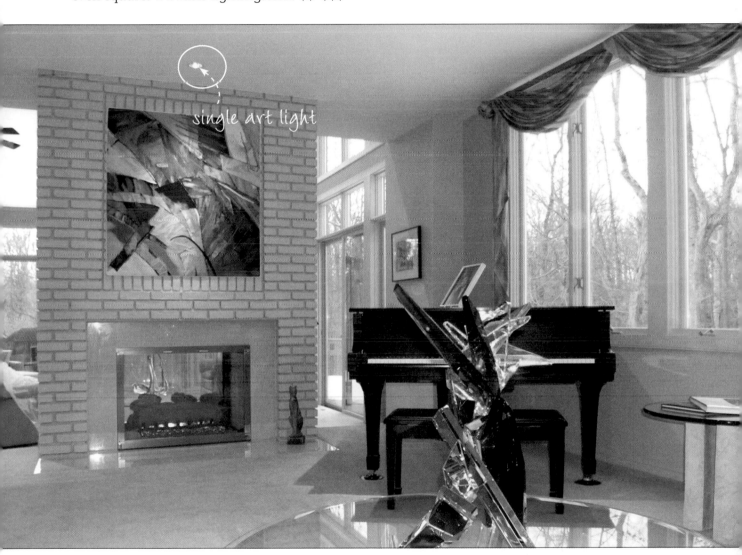

One low-voltage recessed art light over the glass sculpture and one for the wall painting is all this room needed to add drama.

Photo by Designing Solutions

LIGHTING

small recessed adjustable lights

Yep, those are indeed real Megaladon teeth, and to keep the focus and light on all those arti-facts, I used small, low-voltage recessed adjustable lights in the ceiling.
Photo by Mark Finkenstaedt

Control

Lutron: Everything and anything you need to turn lighting on and off, including radio frequency systems that control your lights away from home. Receptacles, too. www.lutron.com. $–$$$

bronze finish
hides spots

Sure, the bronze finish on these lights looks great with the granite, but I really chose them because they'll hide any cooking spots and stains from the cooktop underneath.

Photo by Anne Gummerson

Low-voltage lighting provides the most dramatic room lighting. This option is more expensive to purchase but costs pennies to run.

Photo by Mark Finkenstaedt

LIGHTING

low-voltage lighting

keep stylized
lights on the ceiling

A little bit country or a little bit rock and roll? No matter the style, keep it on the ceiling.
Photo by Mark Finkenstaedt

If you don't want to give your kids remote control lighting, then place a light switch by the bed.

Photo by Mark Finkenstaedt

LIGHTING

Chapter 5

LIVING IN COLOR

If I had a recipe that would tell you exactly what color to paint your room or which colors work best together, I'd be a Nobel Peace Prize winner, saving millions of relationships from falling apart because couples could stop fighting about what color to paint the house. You'd follow my recipe, buy the ingredients, mix them together, put roller and brush to wall, and after a little baking … voilà! The perfect colors, the perfect home, the perfect rooms.

Unfortunately for us both, that recipe doesn't exist. I guess that's why I'm still working and so many homes are done in white, or off-white, or some combination of white with off-white. Without a recipe to follow, most people are afraid of color and argue about color, ultimately settling for off-white. Rooms look bland in off-white, homes eventually look dingy in white, and no one can live a normal life in a white and cream home. It's make believe—and works only in magazines or on TV. We need color.

Photo by Designing Solutions

drab wall color

BEFORE

If choosing colors were as simple as pairing vanilla ice cream with apple pie or milk and chocolate chip cookies, there'd be no reason to read further. But it's not that simple, and that's a big reason why designers like me stay employed; getting color right takes good taste, experience, instinct, and a lot of trial and error. It's such an important design aspect that it warrants professional help. If you're simply not up to the challenge, don't hesitate to hire a color consultant or designer who specializes in color to help you put together a total color plan for your home. But make sure that person follows my rules below so their work will last.

Color is camouflage and your best tool in protecting your home from the people who live in it.

COLOR

bold
wall color

AFTER

Photo by Designing Solutions

red wall color
hides fingerprints!

Inspired by the artwork and stair runner, there was no problem convincing this client to paint her foyer a rich red. Besides, strong color on a stair wall does a great job of hiding fingerprints.
Photo by Mark Finkenstaedt

Color is camouflage and your best tool in protecting your home from the people who live in it. You need to know where and how to use it; it's not as simple as covering every wall and ceiling in mud-colored brown paint! I look closely at the spots, shedding hair, and wall marks in my clients' homes. With kids, I pay close attention to stair walls, the place that attracts the most

fun walls
for kids!

It's hard to tell the kid from the wall!
Photo by Mark Finkenstaedt

COLOR

dirty handprints, and use a stronger paint color there. With shedding pets, I pay close attention to the floor so that pet hair blends in to the rugs. With husbands, I just try not to pay attention: hope for the best but prepare for the worst.

To Thine Own Self Be True, or Go with Your Gut

Even with these considerations in your head, you first have to figure out what you like—what really appeals to you. Color has to be *more* than camouflage; it has to make design sense and make you happy, all at the same time. Your home should be decorated with colors you love, so you're the one who has to choose it.

A client who deals with highly scientific legal matters likes blue. Blue dominates her master bedroom, and it took some convincing to get her comfortable with adding another color to cut down all the blue—yellow. The less the room colors deviated from one another, the more comfortable she was.

A colorful broken-tile backsplash, ceramic tile flooring, and rug keep my friend Ellen's kitchen looking as spotless as it does now ... even after the kids make dinner!
Photos by Mark Finkenstaedt

colorful broken tile backsplash

ceramic floor

Photo by Mark Finkenstaedt

yellow makes blue and white pop!

Photo by Anne Gummerson

different shot of room

COLOR

Adding golden yellow walls with white bedding makes my client's favorite color, blue, stand out even more.

A free-spirit client who wore some of the funkiest jewelry I ever saw liked to mix things up. We chose purple for the crown molding and peach and pale periwinkle for the walls; and black and orange for the upholstery. Nothing matched exactly, but it all blended beautifully to give a great, finished look and a very stimulating first floor of her house.

Getting the color right takes good taste, experience, instinct and a lot of trial and error.

painted table legs hide messes

The green base on the butcher-block table and stools does a great job of concealing scratches and dings caused by the kids who sit at the table.

Photo by Mark Finkenstaedt

An awkward space under a sloped ceiling looks better with subtly colored striping.

Photo by Mark Finkenstaedt

A genealogist client chose colors that camouflaged the constantly shedding hair of her cherished dog, a golden Labradoodle. She liked using bold golden colors but wanted only geometric patterns—straight lines were her preference. We stayed away from abstracts, instead painting stripes on her kitchen walls.

The collection of cabbage-leaf dishes led to garden-themed dining chairs that will never show a spot or stain!

Photo by Barbara Sweeney

inspired from cabbage plates

COLOR

One client had her dining room walls painted in a deep purple—almost grape—before she hired me. My job was to add even more purple throughout the living room and foyer. While it's much harder to decorate a large living area around one room's dark, deep wall color, purple was her muse and we stuck with it through the first floor. Once you know yourself and your own personal comfort zone, you're taking your first steps in the right direction.

If you can identify your favorite colors, use them all—on trim, on accent walls, on the ceiling, and in the furnishings.
Photo by Stacey Zarin

purple used on trim

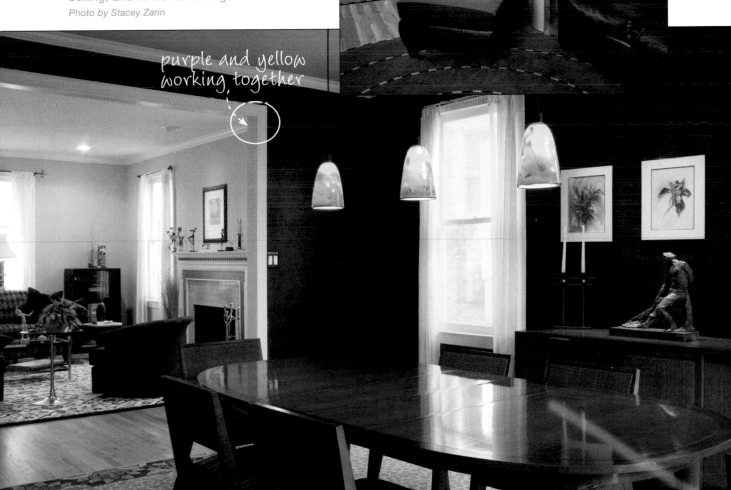

purple and yellow working together

Any color can be made to work anywhere—as long as you like it.
Photo by Anne Gummerson

Building a Color Plan Is Like Assembling a Layer Cake

My family loves to eat. We may be just a party of four when we go out to a restaurant, but we order for eight and tip accordingly. Servers love us! So it's no wonder I like to use food analogies to describe essential steps in home design.

A good layer cake has delicious filling, fabulous icing, and, most important, many layers of great cake. To get started, you need to have a bottom layer of cake. That's your floor. Find your rug, your carpet, your hardwood or tile, and choose wisely so that the flooring provides the durability and camouflage needed for your lifestyle and comes in a color that fits your taste and makes you happy. You'll be seeing a lot of this color—flooring goes everywhere in your home, and in Chapter 1, I gave my top tips for getting the floor just right. If your furniture is a solid color—brown leather or navy chenille—you can add more color and pattern in the rug to help make the solid furniture stand out and keep the room from looking boring. If the furniture fabric is vibrant, subtle flooring in a simple pattern is a better complement.

COLOR

Just a little striping and stenciling with color goes a long way to calling attention to areas and architectural features you want to highlight.
Photo on left by Mark Finkenstaedt
Photos on right by Barbara Sweeney

stripes

The point is, the color of your flooring is your first layer of cake. For filling between layers, use your upholstery fabric so that they work together and complement each other. Take samples in a baggie when you go shopping so that you can see fabric samples with carpet samples. Take all the samples with you when you shop for window fabrics, accessories, and, ultimately, paint. The baggie should reflect the colors and patterns you really prefer and want to see most when you're in the rooms of your home. If you're putting fabric shades or some kind of covering on the windows, choose them next. The colors you use on your windows are the second layer of cake. You can take two directions with window colors: either use the same flavor as the first layer of cake and filling— your floor and seating—or add a new flavor altogether:

1 If you want to really emphasize your windows and make a design statement, the fabric can be dramatic. Your eye will be drawn beyond your seating area to the window.

2 If you just want to add some privacy to your windows without making a big deal or stealing attention from your seating area, keep the material on the windows simple. Your focus will remain more on the colorful upholstery fabric and rug.

COLOR

all the patterns
go together

patterns in
harmony

Paint—The Icing on the Cake

Choosing paint colors for walls, trim, and ceilings isn't where you start in room design; it's where you finish … most of the time. Unless your room is deliberately bare and devoid of furniture, choose the paint colors to complement everything else in the room. Paint is the icing on the cake—it finishes your masterpiece and is chosen to make all the other ingredients taste and look better. Look past the chair covered in your favorite fabric. Is the wall behind it painted to make the chair look better? It should be.

painted banister

If you can't replace a builder-grade white banister, paint it so it won't show fingerprints!

Photo by Anne Gummerson

It's All About Synergy

Synergy means, literally, that the whole is greater than the sum of the parts. In a cake, it means that each layer, each filling between the layers, and the icing on top all combine to create an orgasmic taste in each forkful. (I'm old, I've been married a long time, and cake works for me now.) A piece of cake tastes better than a taste of each individual layer all by itself. That's synergy. And as soon as I get my head out of the fridge, I'll tell you how this translates in home design.

colors for the room come from rug

Tomato red and mustard yellow, pulled right from the runner, balance each other in a tight space. I chose where to put the red and the gold carefully—so the little hall looks bigger, not smaller.
Photo by Anne Gummerson

Even soft, serene colors can speak volumes in the right combination.
Photo by Mark Finkenstaedt

COLOR

We want each element in each room in your home to work together seamlessly to create one perfect space. Sure, the windows are covered in gorgeous fabric, the rug is amazing, and the seating is one-of-a-kind, but it all works as one, combined together in a room. Like a puzzle, each individual piece of the room doesn't make much sense alone. If you interlock the pieces, the picture becomes clear. Color works the same way. Put the strongest shades and patterns just where you need them most—on flooring, upholstery, windows or walls. Wherever you need the most camouflage, that's where to add your largest pieces of the puzzle. Here's help with all those puzzle pieces:

Photo by Designing Solutions

BEFORE

stripe below molding draws eye up

AFTER

The oversize crown molding just didn't cut it in white, so I added a blue stripe to echo the sofa and artwork. By drawing your eye up to the ceiling, it makes the room seem taller.

Photo by Morgan Howarth

Choosing paint colors for walls, trim, and ceilings is not where you start in room design, it's where you finish.

white walls are cold and boring

BEFORE

Photo by Designing Solutions

From one room to the next, the colors repeat, complement, and build to create rooms that flow and work together. The stronger colors were added to the room the kids use most.

Photo by Mark Finkenstaedt

COLOR

yellow warms the room up

blue wash on the fireplace

AFTER

I had the fireplace's concrete washed in blue so the embedded stones would stand out. The only thing missing—Gumby figures scaling the walls!

Photo by Randy Sager

In your home, we want each element in your room to work together seamlessly to create one perfect space.

no color is very drab

BEFORE

Photo by Designing Solutions

COLOR

Guidelines for Choosing Paint Colors

1. For a more serene and calming feeling, paint walls to match the dominant color in your seating and flooring. Monotone rooms or rooms with just two or three similar, repeating colors are classic.

2. Trim that's painted the same as walls, or in a shade very similar to walls, gives a more subtle look to rooms. The trim blends in and gives a continuous look to windows, flooring, and door openings.

3. To make furnishings stand out, paint walls in color(s) that contrast with the upholstery or flooring.

4. To make your ceiling seem higher, choose a ceiling color that contrasts with your

serene foyer

Photo by Designing Solutions

everything is brightened with matching color, curtains, and accents

AFTER

From the curtain trim to the green stripe on the crown molding, to the dining chair and sofa fabric, and even to the toss pillow and Art Deco painting behind it, all the colors and patterns fit together like a puzzle.

Photo by Morgan Howarth

walls. I especially like a pale, cool blue. It contrasts beautifully with warmer wall colors and gives a "sky" effect to your ceiling.

5 To make high ceilings seem lower and rooms cozier, use a ceiling color that's darker and more dramatic.

room looks cavernous

darker ceiling makes room cozy

BEFORE

AFTER

Photos by Designing Solutions

6 White trim makes wall color look fresher. It makes wall and floor colors pop by providing a sharp, contrasting separation between walls, windows, floors, doors, and ceiling. It's what we're most used to seeing in homes.

Photo by Mark Finkenstaedt

COLOR

Photo by Anne Gummerson

Plus, it's easy to touch up white trim with Wite-Out.

7 When I get stuck, I choose a shade of blue—any shade of blue. Even if blue isn't my favorite color, I know I like some shades of blue; everyone does. It's the most popular color in America, and it's used in some way, in some shade, in almost every home. Blue, or water, mixes well with every other color, be it yellow, black, brown, red, orange—whatever. Blue is always a safe choice for adding color.

When I'm stuck, I often turn to a shade of blue—used here in the cabinetry and in the chaise.
Photo by Anne Gummerson

Can you really do this? If you've got time and good taste, yes! Even when you hire a pro, there's a lot of hit and miss. The perfect color in the paint store or magazine is rarely the perfect color in your home. Lighting changes how wall color looks—both the lighting you added from the previous chapter and the natural lighting coming through your windows. What you put on the windows also affects how wall color will look in your home. Shades and blinds filter the natural light and will lighten or darken your walls. Don't come home with gallons of paint based on a color chip in the store; you've got to try it out at home. The color will look different in the day than it does at night. Put a sample of color up on the wall and view it at both times of day to be certain you really like it all the time.

Once you've got the color just right in one room, the next room is just as important.

cold and gray

bright and warm

matches the back wall

Photo by Designing Solutions

Photo by Randy Sager

The View from the Room

Once you've got the color just right in one room, the next room is just as important. When I'm doing a color plan, I stand at one end of the house and look through each doorway, opening, and hall to the next room. The wall color I use in the hall or around a door is the "frame" to the next room, and my goal is to get each room perfectly framed to look its best. Just like the baggie full of floor and fabric samples—puzzle pieces that synergistically combine to make a great color palette—place all your paint chips together, one next to the other, to make certain that room's color works with the next room's. All the colors should combine, from one room to the next, like a puzzle, giving one perfect, finished home.

red from wall repeated on mantel

The red on the wall outside this living room is repeated in the fireplace, drawing the eye through the door-way and to the mantel.

Photo by Mark Finkenstaedt

squash color walls
lead to pumpkin
sitting area

COLOR

Photo by Randy Sager

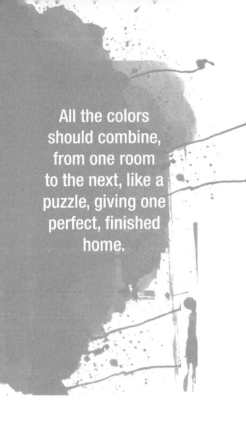

All the colors should combine, from one room to the next, like a puzzle, giving one perfect, finished home.

The soft mustard-yellow doorway frames the adjoining pale peach room.
Photo by Designing Solutions

soft mustard

pale peach

darker version

lighter room

A soft, apricot-colored dining room leads to a stronger, peach-colored library.
Photo by Designing Solutions

COLOR

Lasting Paint Finishes

Which paint finish to choose was once an important consideration. Everyone wanted industrial-strength paint that could withstand a jackhammer. With today's greener paint formulas that cover in just two coats, even flat, matte-finish paints are truly scrubbable, meaning you can remove most spots without removing the paint as well. This is particularly good news because most homes have imperfections— settlement cracks, nail pops, and other drywall blemishes—that will stand out more when there's a sheen to your wall paint. The flatter, more matte the paint, the better the coverage of those imperfections. The same is true for ceilings.

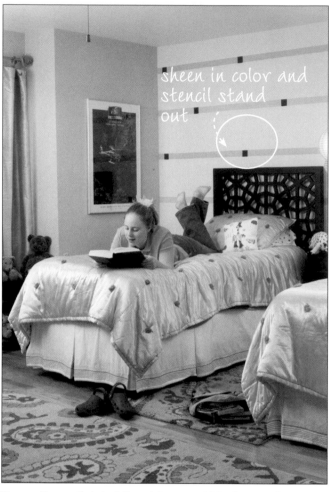

The walls are flat, but the stripes and black stencils have a slight sheen so that they stand out more than the green background color.
Photo by Mark Finkenstaedt

Wood trim on moldings and doors does look better with a glossy sheen. Semigloss paint for trim is a happy medium, providing just enough light-reflecting sheen to stand out and yet not too much that you'll see seams between pieces of molding. Glossy paint is also better protection for wood surfaces because they'll need an occasional scrub to stay looking good.

When clients are desperate, I have two tricks up my sleeve that bring some sanity to choosing the most durable wall paint. First, I use Benjamin Moore AquaPearl paint finish on the walls. This is the same formula used in cafeterias, hospitals, and other commercial settings where the walls really take a beating and need constant scrubbing. My philosophy is that if you feel your family belongs in an institution, paint the walls with institutional-grade paint. AquaPearl provides a hard, durable wall coating with a mild, pearlescent sheen that's the perfect choice for, say, a baby's room, once your child learns that he can take off his own dirty diaper and throw it across the room. You can look around your home and immediately see the problem areas: doors, stair walls, bathrooms. If you can already see chips and fingerprints on the walls and base trim, use AquaPearl when you repaint.

If you are resorting to AquaPearl paint, you need to know about its glossier companion—AquaGlo—for the trim. It has just enough sheen for your moldings and trim, with the institutional properties you need for durability. I assure you, from years of personal experience, these paints will allow you to get *anything* off the walls.

My second trick? Choose wall colors that match permanent ink markers. Really. Why is this highlighted? I can't remember! Leave it as is. I touch up walls, even furniture with permanent ink markers all the time. Why? Many people, like myself, have amateur decorators at home that may, for example, hang their football team's poster on your living room wall days before the Superbowl. When it's time to redecorate on the Monday after the Superbowl, you may inadvertently remove the paint along with the poster you're tossing in the garbage. A marker, matched to the wall paint, will provide a quick and immediate fix without rummaging through the garage to find a can of paint. In my private arsenal at home, I have tons of Wite-Out for touching up trim and every color marker made by Sharpie, all color-coordinated to work with my walls and furniture. It's not that I have to use them daily, but in addition to the Superbowl, I need to use my markers during basketball, baseball, and hockey seasons. And guess what … our teams have made the play-offs!

Favorite Trim Colors, in Semigloss (both work well with Wite-Out):

1. Benjamin Moore White Dove OC-17
2. Benjamin Moore Decorators White

White Dove   Decorators White

Favorite Ceiling Colors, in Flat:

1. Benjamin Moore Cumulus Cotton 2063-70
2. Benjamin Moore Whispering Spring 2136-70
3. Benjamin Moore Patriotic White 2135-70

Cumulus Cotton   Whispering Spring   Patriotic White

Favorite Wall Colors:

Neutrals (Use sparingly):

1. Benjamin Moore Yosemite Sand AC-4
2. Benjamin Moore Desert Tan 2153-50

Yosemite Sand   Desert Tan

3. Benjamin Moore Golden Straw 2152-50

4. Benjamin Moore Putnam Ivory HC-39

Reds and orange:

1. Benjamin Moore Adobe Dust 2175-40

2. Benjamin Moore Soft Pumpkin 2166-40

3. Benjamin Moore Rosy Apple 2006-30

4. Benjamin Moore Adobe Orange 2171-30

5. Benjamin Moore Pink Mix 2089-30

6. Benjamin Moore Rosy Peach 2089-20

Golds:

1. Benjamin Moore Concord Ivory HC-12

2. Benjamin Moore York Harbor Yellow 2154-40

3. Benjamin Moore Golden Tan 2152-40

Blues:

1. Benjamin Moore Soft Chinchilla 2135-50

2. Benjamin Moore Summer Shower 2135-60

3. Benjamin Moore Gossamer Blue 2123-40

4. Benjamin Moore Palladian Blue HC-144

5. Benjamin Moore Woodlawn Blue HC-147

6. Benjamin Moore Wythe Blue HC-143

7. Benjamin Moore Covington Blue HC-138

Greens:

1. Benjamin Moore Hancock Green HC-117

2. Benjamin Moore Fernwood Green 2145-40

3. Benjamin Moore Rosemary Sprig 2144-30

4. Benjamin Moore Brookside Moss 2145-30

5. Benjamin Moore Dill Pickle 2147-40

6. Benjamin Moore Van Alen Green HC-120

7. Benjamin Moore Jalepeño Pepper 2147-30

Golden Straw • Putnam Ivory

Adobe Dust • Soft Pumpkin • Rosy Apple

Adobe Orange • Pink mix • Rosy Peach

Concord Ivory • York Harbor Yellow • Golden Tan

Soft Chinchilla • Summer Shower • Gossamer Blue

Palladian Blue • Woodlawn Blue • Wythe Blue

Covington Blue • Hancock Green • Fernwood Green

Rosemary Sprig • Brookside Moss • Dill Pickle

Van Alen Green • Jalapeño Pepper

COLOR

colors pulled from rug

All pulled from the foyer rug, the teal living room walls work well with the red and gold beyond.
Photo by Designing Solutions

Photo by Stacey Zarin

COLOR

Now you've got a new arsenal of weapons to use against your slobs. No more yelling, no more scrubbing. Instead, follow my design fundamentals to make your home decorating investment last longer.

Think before you choose. You can't retrain the kids to wipe their feet or keep drinks off your coffee table. Your husband will never think to put the toilet seat down (unless you tell him), and the dog will more than likely jump on the sofa as soon as you leave the room. Decorate for the way your family really lives today, and you won't have to worry about how your home will look tomorrow. Let them eat cake … anywhere they like!

Got a designing dilemma in need of a designing solution, or just want to share your ideas about slob-proof design? E-mail me at designer@ mydesigningsolutions.com. I'll do my best to promptly answer your questions and comments.

CONCLUSION

Bookshelves full of collectibles and keepsakes deserve good lighting so that they aren't hidden in shadow created by the shelves themselves. Adjustable recessed lights with halogen bulbs direct the light beam exactly where it's needed most without causing any unwanted glare on the tv. The bright white light keeps the room colors crisp and true.

A highly scrubbable paint, like Benjamin Moore's Regal Matte, camouflages drywall flaws with its flat finish but also withstands abuse from messy hands and daily wear. It's easily scrubbed with a scouring sponge.

Consider weight, weave, and pattern to choose fabrics that will hold up with heavy use and daily wear and tear. When choosing upholstery, start with kiln-dried, screwed, glued, and corner-blocked hardwood for strength and lasting durability. Upgrade seat and back cushions to extend the wear and improve the feel of your chair over time.

Sofa and chair skirts stain quickly from dirty shoes or shedding pets, so consider having an exposed leg on your upholstery and forgoing a skirt. Most manufacturers offer this option.

HOW I DO IT

Photo by Mark Finkenstaedt

Window coverings that go up and down rather than stacking on the sides are better protected from being stepped and pulled on.

For family-friendly family rooms, you can't beat leather. Protected leather, or semianiline leather, has a finish applied to its surface to protect it from staining and spotting. The color is uniform, less likely to fade from sunlight and easy to clean and care for. Its high-durability is perfect for families, pet-owners, or for high-traffic spaces.

Nothing lasts longer or looks better than a well-finished hardwood floor.

A heavily-textured, colorful rug in New Zealand wool holds up in even the highest traffic areas. The wool's high lanolin content keeps spills, spots, and stains from being absorbed into the fibers. Soil remains on the surface until you clean it up.